An Introduction to
GOD

ENCOUNTERING THE DIVINE IN ORTHODOX CHRISTIANITY

Andrew Stephen Damick

ANCIENT FAITH PUBLISHING ✢ CHESTERTON, INDIANA

An Introduction to God:
Encountering the Divine in Orthodox Christianity
Copyright © 2014 Andrew Stephen Damick

Scripture quotations are taken from the New King James Version,
© 1979, 1980, 1982 by Thomas Nelson, Inc. Used by permission.

Published by:
    Ancient Faith Publishing
    A Division of Ancient Faith Ministries
    P.O. Box 748
    Chesterton, IN 46304

ISBN: 978-1-936270-99-6

Printed in the United States of America

Cover design by Symbology Creative
Cover photo copyright iStock Photography. Used with permission.

20 19 18 17 16   13 12 11 10 9 8 7 6 5 4 3 2

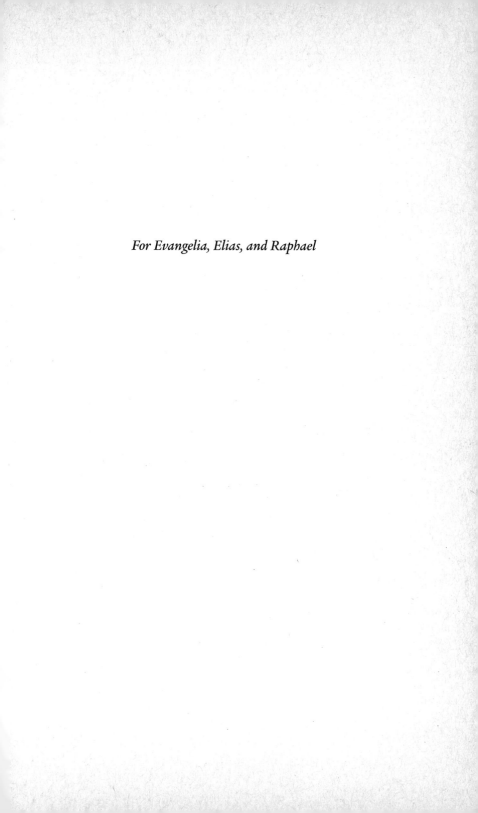

For Evangelia, Elias, and Raphael

Contents

I know very well when, but hardly how, the final step was taken. I was driven to Whipsnade one sunny morning. When we set out I did not believe that Jesus is the Son of God and when we reached the zoo I did.

—C. S. Lewis

Preface & Acknowledgments

I had a hard time figuring out how to get into this book. The starting texts were a set of four lectures entitled *Foundations of the Orthodox Faith*, a parish education series presenting core, primal questions concerning Orthodox Christianity. This book represents a significant rewrite and recasting of the themes explored in those lectures. Its present form arose from a desire to present that same core of Orthodox Christian explorations to an un-churched, ex-churched, or de-churched audience (however one wants to define those terms). I hope it will also be profitable to people who already have a connection to Jesus Christ, because I believe committed Christians have reason to engage with these issues, as well. And some people are in church yet are not sure why they're there. This book is for them, too.

But why was it hard to get into the writing of this book? At some point during the process of its conception, I had arrived upon the title *An Introduction to God*, and that appealed to me. But I didn't realize that my conception of what that title would present was essentially informational: How do I convey the *data* about God? How do I teach someone "God"? I couldn't figure out an answer to these questions, especially when I considered my intended audience of people who had either never had any association with Christ or had perhaps drifted away or rejected church life.

The point at which the book finally made sense to me was when I had the opportunity to ask a new friend, an actor and musician who was in the process of being received into the Orthodox Church, what he would say to his fans, what message he would give them about Orthodoxy if he could sit down and talk to them about it. I fully expected a sort of "elevator speech" in response—a slogan or one-paragraph summary to attempt to hook them into buying into Orthodoxy.

What I got instead rather surprised and even shamed me. His response was not an "elevator speech." Instead, the first thing he said to me was that such an encounter would have to be preceded by intercession. What would he say to his fans? He would first have to *pray for them*. Why? Because he was not there to explain God to them. Rather, he wanted to provide them space for an *encounter*. In other words, he wanted to introduce them to God.

That's what shamed me. Why? There I was, well into my second decade of being an Orthodox Christian—and a clergyman and pastor, to boot—and I had just had the core

of Orthodox evangelism communicated to me by a cate-
chumen, someone who was a beginner in the faith. I had
become so convinced that I needed to *explain* God, to provide an introduction to the *subject* of God—contrary to the
whole attitude of Orthodox Christian theology—but what
is actually needed is an introduction to God Himself, just
as you might introduce one friend to another. And thus it
was through that encounter that the subtitle for this work
occurred to me, *Encountering the Divine in Orthodox Christianity*, because the introduction to Orthodoxy is really an
encounter with God, and because that extended encounter
is what Orthodox Christianity actually is.

My hope, therefore, is that, whether you know Him
already or not, this book will serve in some way to make possible a true introduction (or re-introduction) to God, that
it will provide or clear out some sacred space in which the
encounter between you and the Divine One can occur. After
all, as my friend said to me later, Jesus did not say, "*This* is
the way, the truth, and the life"; He said, "*I* am the way, the
truth, and the life."

For that critical and insightful reminder, I am grateful
to Jonathan Jackson (the new friend mentioned above), who
also graciously wrote the foreword for this book. I am also
grateful to those who read this manuscript while it was still
in process and gave helpful criticisms and suggestions.

In particular, I give thanks to my friend Michael Lands-
man, who offered comments from outside the Orthodox

tradition yet sympathetic to it, as well as to Anna Pougas, who helped me see what it was like to be raised with Orthodoxy yet not know it intimately and then later come to fuller faith. I am also indebted to Dr. Daniel G. Opperwall, who gave extensive comments on the manuscript that revealed some of its larger flaws, which I've tried to correct. I'm grateful to my old friend and godbrother Andrew Hall, who has shown me how to keep fighting to live the faith even when it sometimes makes no sense.

My thanks also go to the folks at Ancient Faith Publishing, who, upon receiving the original version of this manuscript, saw that it could be something better than it was and have helped in the editing to make it so.

To my family goes special gratitude, especially to my parents, Bill and Sandy Damick, who gave me my introduction to God. I am grateful to my three children, Evangelia, Elias, and Raphael, who playfully and joyfully (and even, sometimes, patiently) receive their parents' attempts to introduce them to God—and who also in turn introduce us to God. And I am most especially thankful to my wife, Khouriyeh* Nicole, whose sacrifices, love, and forgiveness keep introducing me to God in the most enduring and compelling ways possible.

Finally, I wish to say something about the act of thanksgiving itself, especially regarding the God to whom I hope

---

* An honorific title for a priest's wife in the Arabic Orthodox tradition.

to introduce you. I once received criticism for not explicitly thanking God in a previous work, and the thought that occurred to me in response is that I should not thank God for my writings. Why? In some sense, it is somehow to blame Him for what I produce, with all of its imperfections. I also cannot with any honesty claim some sort of special divine inspiration for my writing. I can, however, thank God for what He has done for me and what He is doing for you. So if, in any way, what I have written has participated in that introduction and encounter for you, I am grateful to Him for that.

Fr. Andrew Stephen Damick
Emmaus, Pennsylvania
May 2014

Foreword

The title of this book, *An Introduction to God,* presupposes that the reader is interested in being introduced to God. Therefore, if you are holding this book in your hands with the intent of reading it, you are most likely a seeker. Whether you have consciously known Christ since childhood or never professed any faith at all, you are intent on being introduced to God, or perhaps re-introduced to Him. What exciting and awe-inspiring possibilities lie ahead!

Fr. Andrew Damick has written a beautiful, humble, and profound book on the mystery of God's love for mankind. It is beautiful because the author is introducing the reader to the Beautiful One. It is humble because Fr. Andrew has no interest in conveying his own ideas or philosophies—only the True Faith as passed down from Christ and His Apostles from generation to generation. It is profound because it is a clear and prayerful exposition of pristine Christianity.

There is a story in the Book of Acts where the Apostle Philip is told by the Holy Spirit to join the chariot of a certain Ethiopian eunuch. "So Philip ran to him, and heard him reading the prophet Isaiah, and said, 'Do you understand what you are reading?' And he said, 'How can I, unless someone guides me?' And he asked Philip to come up and sit with him" (Acts 8:30–31). The apostle went on to interpret the Scriptures and proclaim the Gospel to him. The Ethiopian man was overwhelmed and desired to be baptized at once. The Apostle Philip introduced this man to God, the Lover of Mankind.

This story is a vivid portrayal of our need for humility. The Ethiopian eunuch was meek and poor in spirit; he was not puffed up or arrogant, believing himself capable of interpreting the Scriptures on his own, through private revelation. His response to the apostle can become ours as well, if only we receive the grace and humility to do as he did. We should be ready to say, "How can I understand, unless someone guides me?" and continuously invite the Apostles and the Fathers of the Church to sit with us and teach us how to interpret the Scriptures and live the authentic Gospel.

It is indeed "a fearful thing to fall into the hands of the living God" (Heb. 10:31). Thus, it is with great humility that the author approaches this work—the work of introducing us to God. In *An Introduction to God*, Fr. Andrew opens the heart and mind to the Holy Tradition of the Orthodox

Church, introducing us to the beauty of the Holy Trinity. It is a faith steeped in mystery, grace, and love.

I am immensely grateful to have been introduced to Fr. Andrew and to call him my friend. He is a man of deep reflection, warmth, and humor. I am eager for this incredible book to be shared with the world! Even now, in this moment, the Lover of Mankind says, "Behold, I stand at the door and knock. If anyone hears My voice and opens the door, I will come in to him and dine with him, and he with Me" (Rev. 3:20).

Jonathan Jackson
Nashville, Tennessee
November 2013

The Gospel

Jesus Christ is the Messiah. He rose from the dead. Humanity can therefore be saved.

Those three sentences constitute the core narrative of the Gospel, the *good news* according to the Orthodox Christian faith. Orthodox Christians have affirmed this story as a sacred history for twenty centuries, and entering into this story is what constitutes the spiritual life for us. I know you may not believe any of this, but I include it here because this sacred history is what's in the background for this book. The following is a basic outline of that history. Giving it here is not meant to be a didactic lecture but rather to explain what is the core of the Orthodox Christian story, which informs everything we are.

In the beginning, God created the universe,[†] including mankind, whom He placed at the center of the creation. He created us to live forever, without sickness, suffering, or death, and in perfect, ever-deepening communion with Him. But because Adam and Eve, the first parents of mankind, chose to sin—to miss the mark of God's design for them—corruption and death entered into man. This is called the "Fall of mankind." And because mankind was chosen by God to act as the priest of this world—offering up the creation to God and then receiving it back as a means of blessing—the creation also fell away from the harmonious peace God had designed for it. This happened because God is the Giver of life and the Creator of order, so when humanity cut itself off from God, death and chaos were introduced into humanity and, through us, into the rest of the world.

Over time, as corruption and death touched everything mankind did, the world came to be ruled by violence and oppression. God began a process of revealing to humanity the way out of this corruption, the way to reconnection with the life of God. He did this first through a man He chose especially for this task, Abraham, and then by giving a way of life to Abraham's descendants, who were first called Hebrews and then later Jews. God spoke to these chosen people first through the Prophet Moses and then through other prophets.

---

† Orthodoxy makes no definitive statement about exactly how God created the universe or in what amount of time. The important point is that He did create it *ex nihilo*, out of nothing.

To Moses, God revealed that He was to be known to the Hebrews as *Yahweh*, which means "I am." This showed that the way of life He was revealing was intended to enable people to know who God is, not just intellectually, but in a true and personal way. This way of life revealed through Moses had only one purpose: to teach the Hebrews and the nations around them how to get back in connection with God so that they could truly know Him. And He showed Himself to Israel not only as their deity, but as their Father, which spoke of His desire for an intimate and close connection. Over the centuries that followed Abraham and Moses, the nation of the Jews, called Israel, was sometimes faithful to God but often lost its way.

About two thousand years ago, a young virgin named Mary, a descendant of David, the greatest of the kings of the Jews, was betrothed to an old, pious man named Joseph, also a descendant of David. Because of her purity of heart and her willingness to do as God asked her to do, she was chosen by God to give birth to the Son of God, Jesus Christ. She willingly assented to this pregnancy, which was announced to her by the Archangel Gabriel, and the One born of her was called Jesus, which means "Yahweh saves."

Jesus was not only the Son of the Father but was also God Himself, and He revealed that God is the Holy Trinity—Father, Son, and Holy Spirit, three divine Persons who share one essence, one God in three Persons. And when Jesus was conceived in Mary's womb—miraculously, without any earthly father—He who had been fully God also became fully human, taking His humanity from her. Because of who Jesus was (and is), both God and man, humanity has the possibility of being restored to full communion with God. Through His humanity, we can access His divinity. The gap opened by Adam and Eve has been bridged.

During His ministry on Earth, Jesus taught the people the way God wants us to live, healed them of their physical and spiritual sicknesses, and forgave them of their sins. He especially focused His ministry on twelve disciples, who were not members of the religious or intellectual classes but mostly fishermen. When His mission drew to a close, He was betrayed by Judas, one of these twelve, and was arrested by the Roman authorities. The Romans were acting on behalf of the religious leadership of the Jews, who saw Jesus as a threat to their established order. Although He had done nothing wrong, He was convicted as a blasphemer and crucified—nailed to a large wooden cross to suffocate to death—by the Roman imperial government on behalf of the Jewish leaders.

Jesus died on a Friday, the day before the Jews' greatest annual holy day, the Passover, a day that commemorated the delivery of the Hebrew people from slavery in Egypt. Jesus rose from the dead on the third day, Sunday. Through this voluntary death and resurrection, Jesus broke the power of death over all mankind forever. After His resurrection, He was seen alive by many, including the eleven disciples (Judas, in his remorse for betraying Christ, had meanwhile committed suicide) and many others. He spent another forty days on Earth, further instructing His eleven disciples to help them become *apostles,* a word which means "those sent out on a mission." After those forty days, He physically ascended into heaven while the apostles watched.

The apostles, following the instructions Jesus gave them, began to travel throughout the known world, preaching the Gospel everywhere, telling anyone who would listen the good news and baptizing them into the name of the Father, Son, and Holy Spirit. This good news is that, by repenting of sins (turning away from all the ways we miss the perfection God created us for) and being baptized into membership in the Church—which Jesus Himself called His "Body"—it is possible for a person to conquer death, just as Jesus did through His sacrifice on the cross. We can make the passage into death a passage into resurrection, because incorporation into the ongoing life of the Church is participation in Christ. This is what it means to be "saved."

Someday, Jesus will return again, and time as we know it will end. Everyone will be resurrected bodily at the end of time, but only those who are "in Christ" will be raised to a resurrection of eternal life with God. Those who reject Christ and do not partake of what He offered will be raised to a resurrection of judgment. This judgment is essentially a continuation of existence cut off from the life that God gives—dying eternally instead of living eternally.

Jesus therefore is the fulfillment, the full revelation of all that God began through Abraham and Moses, showing a way of life that made possible direct communion with God. The Church is therefore also the fulfillment of the chosen community that was ancient Israel, a real community of people called to live in harmony together, communing with God and each other through the primary means God provided for His presence to be manifested among His people: the holy mysteries, also called *sacraments*. These sacraments include baptism, the Eucharist (also called the Lord's Supper or Holy Communion), marriage, and others.

The apostles were the first to administer these mysteries in the Church. Part of their ministry was to ordain the next generation of Christian leaders as bishops. These bishops in turn ordained presbyters (priests) and deacons to help them with the work. As the Gospel spread throughout the world, new bishops were ordained by the apostles and their successors to lead the Church, which will continue its work until its fulfillment when Jesus returns at the end of time.

Jesus founded only one Church to be His Body, not the multitude of competing Christian denominations we see in our own day. Only one Church has maintained that continuous existence through all the centuries since the Resurrection of Christ, teaching and believing and living the same Christian life throughout history. That Church is the Orthodox Church.

Orthodox Christians do not know the fate of those who

believe in Christ yet belong to groups that have broken away from the historic Orthodox Church. We know only that we must be faithful to what we have received so that we may pass it on to the next generation, to anyone who will hear and believe.

This is the core of what Orthodox Christians believe. The rest of this book proceeds from this essential Gospel story. It is an attempt to grapple with some of the primary difficulties people encounter when trying to access this story.

CHAPTER ONE

Entering the Mystery

Where Is God?

Then Moses said to God, "Indeed, when I come to the children of Israel and say to them, 'The God of your fathers has sent me to you,' and they say to me, 'What is His name?' what shall I say to them?"

Exodus 3:13

What do I say to someone who has no idea who Jesus Christ is? What do I say to someone who doesn't really care who He is? What do I say to someone who's spent some time in church but doesn't want anything to do with it any more? What do I say to someone who's in church but isn't really sure why she's there?

Even though I am by profession a Christian pastor and

have been a Christian all my life, those questions haunt me. There are days when I think I've got the answers down, and then there are days when I feel helpless. There are even days when *I* am the "someone" on the other side of those questions.

The purpose of this work is not to give an introduction to the *subject* of God, nor even to the subject and facts of Orthodox Christianity—the faith that is believed and lived by the Orthodox Church, the original and most ancient of all Christian churches. Other books serve that purpose quite ably, outlining the facts, structure, history, and detailed dogmatic teachings of the Orthodox (see the annotated bibliography in the back of the book for some suggestions). So what you will find in this book is not a catalog of systematic doctrine, nor is it a narrative of Orthodoxy's path through history—how the Church is organized, all its practices, and so forth.

Rather, as was mentioned in the preface, the aim of this work is to give an introduction to God Himself, to arrange for the reader a meeting with the Creator of all things—and such a meeting should, I hope, be desirable to the reader, since he is one of the Creator's creatures.

But at the same time, as we will explore a bit further below, this book cannot claim to give any positive definitions of exactly who God is. That's not its purpose. Rather, its purpose is to try to enter into a few of the more common arenas of struggle when it comes to trying to get to know God, and having searched these arenas out a bit, find that they can become sacred spaces where God is encountered.

That said, I should of course acknowledge up front that some people simply don't believe in God. I do not know why those people do not believe in God. I wish I did. I also wish I knew why most people *do* believe in God, if only because it might make my job as a Christian pastor—to help people to encounter Him and connect with Him—a bit easier. There does not seem to be any one thread of personality that runs through all atheists or all believers that could give us a clue as to the cause of unbelief or belief. There are skeptics who are believers. There are gullible people who are unbelievers. There are kind-hearted atheists and selfish theists. The rich, the poor, the old, the young, the educated and the uneducated, the majorities and the minorities—none of these seem to have a corner on the market of either belief or unbelief. Perhaps some psychological study might be done that would yield the key to the door that stands between belief and unbelief. But I really do not know where one would begin, if only because "believing in God" can mean many things across the world's religions.

I know people who do not believe in God because they simply see no evidence for God, and because their default position is skepticism, they believe that something for which they have no evidence must not exist. I can respect that position, because it's honest. But deep down, there is no absolute law of human nature that says skepticism is the proper mindset for mankind, that our default attitude can only be disbelief. The skeptic tends to believe that everyone who is not a skeptic must be gullible, but almost no one on Earth really is so credulous as to believe everything he is told. We all tend to form and revise our beliefs with a combination of different measures of trust, investigation, reason, experience, and intuition. The idea that only one of those means of knowing and believing is valid doesn't square with the reality of human life.

All this being the case, I do not know how to *make* someone connect with God, nor what exact combination of trust, investigation, reason, experience, and intuition will produce a believer. Again, I wish I did. But I do know that there *are* believers and that unbelievers sometimes *become* believers—and, of course, sometimes it goes the other way, too. What all believers have in common, at least the ones who really believe and are not faking it, is that they believe God has somehow knocked on the door of their hearts, which is not something that is measurable by psychology or any physical device. This book is therefore written for anyone who believes God has knocked on his door, in whatever way that might mean and whether or not that door has been opened.

This book is also written for people who think God *might* be knocking, but they're not sure. Perhaps they used to believe a long time ago, but through the hypocrisy, cruelty, or betrayal of fake "believers," or through the decay of faith that can so often occur in one's early adult years, or by some other means entirely, they've found themselves on the other side of the line of faith and can no longer say, "I believe."

This book is also written for people who may never have heard God knocking but are wondering if there really is something to this faith business after all. For these people, and for all the others I've mentioned, I propose here to get down to the roots of faith in God, to the primal, core issues that must face everyone who would ask himself, "Do I believe?"

I would also like to invite those who are already Christians into this book, whether they belong to the Orthodox Christian tradition or not. It's not an apologetic work, attempting to convince the reader of the rightness of Orthodox doctrine, but it does explore some of the bigger issues that may lead a Christian to ask himself what he's doing in church, or perhaps what he's doing in the church he's in and whether he should be in that one and not another. What does it mean that God might be knocking, that He might be speaking to you? I have heard many and varying answers to this question from people who say God has spoken to them. Some say it's just a feeling, something they know but can't quite explain. Others say they hear the voice of God in otherwise unexplainable coincidences around them. Some hear His voice through the glory and beauty of creation. Others hear Him in the voices of people they know or in the words of wisdom in a book. There are those who hear God through philosophy and reason. Some find God in music or art. And some say they have seen a miracle.

Whatever the medium for this message from God, I think

we can find the commonality between all these experiences in the fact that each human soul, down in its depths, longs for immortality. Eternity has been put into our hearts. We really cannot imagine what it would be like not to exist. We know death is wrong. We know love is better than hatred. We know beauty really is not merely in the eye of the beholder, but what is beautiful is so without any observation or judgment from us. These things together (and others) reveal to us that at the core of our being, there is a fingerprint left from the Creator, a sort of note from Him letting us know He's looking for that encounter with us, that He's knocking on our door.

So if you are a believer, you really have to ask yourself, "Why am I here?" That is, why do I believe? Why am I in church? What's going on here?

If you're not a believer, you may want to ask the same questions, except putting the word *should* in the right places: "Why *should* I be there?"

If you've never asked yourself those questions, isn't it time you did? These are the big ones, the questions that define what life on Earth really is about. And isn't life—your life— worth that kind of questioning and exploration? Is it not true that the dignity and worth of mankind—even of just one person—is worth the struggle for immortality, for the highest and noblest meaning, the encounter with the living God?

If you ask yourself these questions, and if you truly give them serious exploration—the kind you can be proud of at the end, the kind that makes you sweat, mentally and emotionally, from the exertion—then you will probably find yourself in one of two places.

You could find yourself concluding there really is no God.

Or, after serious, honest exploration, you could find yourself in touch with God. And that's something just a bit scary. But then the adventure really begins.

And where does that adventure begin? It begins with asking what we know about God. Unfortunately, what most of us know about Him is that He seems to be absent.

THE ABSENCE OF GOD

Metropolitan Anthony Bloom (the Russian Orthodox Church's bishop in London from 1957 until his death in 2003), in the opening paragraphs of his book *Beginning to Pray,* directly addresses what may be the most central struggle and disappointment of anyone who has ever contemplated whether there is a God or gods—namely, the absence of God. He writes the following about what it means to begin praying:

> *At the outset there is, then, one very important problem: the situation of one for whom God seems to be absent. This is what I would like to speak about now. Obviously I am not speaking of a real absence—God is never really absent—but of the sense of absence which we have. We stand before God and we shout into an empty sky, out of which there is no reply. We turn in all directions and He is not to be found.[1]*

Is this not so for each of us who has ever wondered whether there is indeed a God? Such thoughts come into the hearts even of those who have believed for their whole lives that God is real and that He loves us. Sometimes, in the dark of the night, or perhaps in the midst of some nightmare of suffering that seems to have no meaning, as Metropolitan Anthony writes, "We stand before God and we shout into an empty sky, out of which there is no reply."

That's happened for me. Being a Christian isn't always a constant, absolute experience of the knowledge of God.

It may well be that you saw the title of this book and thought to yourself, "'An Introduction to God'? But I already know all about God. I'm a Christian!" And of course you are probably right. But I hope you will bear with me if I suggest that, even if you began long ago to get to know God, perhaps you may begin again. You may ask yourself what it means to be introduced to God, what it means to know Him; you may examine these questions as closely to their hearts as you can.

When I first started thinking about how to articulate this exploration, the phrase *an introduction to God* had already stuck in my head. I thought to myself, *Well, how do I introduce God?* God is a subject unlike any other. We could start with the Wikipedia article on God, which as of this writing leads off with this paragraph:

> God is often conceived as the Supreme Being or principal object
> of faith. The concept of God as described by theologians includes

the attributes of omniscience (infinite knowledge), omnipotence (unlimited power), omnipresence (present everywhere), omnibenevolence (perfect goodness), divine simplicity, and eternal and necessary existence.[2]

While that is a rather abstruse piece of prose, and while Wikipedia is not usually considered the most reliable of sources, this is essentially what one would expect in an academic introduction to the subject of God. But in reading such a definition, I find myself stuck, probably because I am not a philosophy professor. Sure, I can define the word *God* and make some comments about what the concept has meant in human history, but for me, at least, there is not much beyond that worth meditating upon. Why? Because it leaves me dry. I have defined the word *God*, and perhaps I have given an introduction to the *subject* of God, but I have not actually introduced God.

This is where we believers in God often trip up when trying to convey our faith to someone who does not share it: We try to define God, to give an introduction to the *subject* of God. As with any other subject, we may try to use proofs for its existence, whether philosophical or evidential. We explain God. We describe God. We make appeals to authoritative texts and persons; to the popularity of belief in God, whether current or historical; to personal emotional experiences. We attempt to impart to our listeners some information about God. But we have not actually introduced God. God is not a subject (nor an object).

After all, if I am speaking with someone who genuinely does not believe in God, none of those proofs or explanations will actually matter. Even if I could produce an incontrovertible argument or undeniable evidence for God's existence, even if I could pull God out of my pocket and show Him to the unbeliever, there is absolutely nothing to prevent him from simply not believing me. He could say the argument is unconvincing, the evidence does not mean what I think it does, or what I have in my pocket is just mildly interesting lint and not the divine presence.

Yet the hunger for truth, the hunger for an introduction to God, is everywhere. Let me give you an example. I often look at the search engine terms people use to find my website. One that especially caught my eye once was this question: "Is there any true religion?"

It is monumental and perhaps even personally pivotal that someone should ask himself that question. But I think it also marks a kind of desperation or despair that he would set about searching for its answer on the internet. "Is there any true religion?" echoes as a cry spoken into the dark, perhaps hoping that somewhere, among the search results, *there* will be the answer.

People are looking for the truth. They are looking for an introduction to God.

Everyone is—even believers. If I am a believer, especially if I am a church-goer, what is the basis for my belief, for my participation in church? Do I really know God? Have I sensed His absence? Have I been introduced to Him? Have I actually met Him? Why am I here?

And where is God, anyway?

In some ways, it is a peculiarly modern problem, this sense of God's absence, that we are missing Him—which is not quite the same as merely not sensing His presence. You can be with someone yet not know it. It's one thing not to see someone around, but another to miss him. But taking human history as a whole, relatively few people anywhere at any time have questioned that there is some God or gods—"a divinity that shapes our ends, rough-hew them how we will," as Shakespeare's Hamlet puts it. Gods and demons and sprites and elves and faeries and spirits—all of these things were quite real to our forebears. They knew for certain not merely that they "believed in" such things, but that they had real evidence for their existence, that they interacted with them, that such beings were a normal, everyday part of life.

To help us understand this, let us consider one of the greatest of the feasts of the Christian year, the Annunciation—that moment when the invisible, immaterial God becomes incarnate as a human child in the womb of the Virgin Mary, at the announcement of the Archangel Gabriel. So what does this feast have to do with former generations' sense of the reality of the divine? It is because the world into which God chose to become incarnate was not one that didn't think He was "out there."

The first-century Jewish context of Jesus' conception was

one that believed there was a God who had been known and experienced by the Jews for centuries. Likewise, the intellectuals among the Greeks and Romans who surrounded the Jews had basically settled on monotheism by then, despite the continuance of polytheism in the broader culture. But what they all had in common was the idea that God was "above," that He was "beyond" this world, that the created, material world was something unworthy of the divine presence.

Even though Jesus was not born into a world of atheists and skeptics, He was nevertheless conceived at a time when the idea of God being conceived—that is, conceived in a woman's womb—was, well, inconceivable. What happened at the Annunciation was utter foolishness to both the Jew and the Greek. For the Jews, God would never become a *man*, and for the Greeks and other Gentiles, God would not only not become a man, He certainly wouldn't become a *Jewish* man! In the eyes of the citizens of Rome, the Jews were a subjugated people, not remotely worthy of such a divine manifestation.

But nevertheless, the Christian revolution began at that moment. And if the coming of God as a material being into this world was an unbelievable and shocking claim in the first century, it is perhaps all the more shocking now. The revolution continues, because in our own time, our sense of things like metaphysics and religion and philosophy has simply expanded upon that sense present in the first century, that God is detached from this world. If, for them, God was forever above this material world, properly high in His heaven, then for this time, God has left this material world entirely, never to return—if He was ever here in the first place.

But as Christians see it, the inconceivable actually happened: God became man. He was and remains *incarnate*, a term that has its origins in the Latin word for "meat." God became meat; He became flesh. He became visible and material—touchable. The separation is over. In our loss and disappointment and separation, God Himself chose to overcome the divide between us so that we might encounter Him, because He loves us and wants to connect with us—all of us—no matter who we are or what we may have done.

The problem remains, though, that introducing people to God is not quite like introducing them to your friends or your family. For one thing, you can't *make* it happen. You can't just summon God and someone else (or yourself) together to set up the introduction. This is also not a casual introduction. This is God. If an introduction to God is going to take place, then the space in which it happens has to be prepared. It has to be sketched out and perhaps even cleared of clutter.

And so, in a sense, this book actually cannot accomplish what it apparently sets out to do—that is, to provide an introduction to God. Rather, its purpose is to make ready the space in which that introduction can happen by dealing with certain core questions that might otherwise impede it. Preparation is critical, because meeting God is different from meeting other people.

In meeting God, you are not there to sit down and have a drink with Him or to chat about politics or television or how the kids are doing in school (though I suppose you could). You are there to connect and unite with the Creator of heaven and Earth—in Orthodox Christian terms, to be transformed, to participate in the dynamic energies of the divine. So this kind of meeting won't work in the casual, distracted, hurried space our hearts usually inhabit.

We have to inhabit a different kind of space. Our hearts have to be prepared for this meeting if it's going to happen. God, of course, is constantly at work preparing the space for our introduction to Him. We cannot imagine how much energy He puts into nudging our lives in this direction or that, even nudging the course of history, in order to set up meetings with Him. But like any meeting, it also depends on us.

So what I propose to do in this book is to clear some sacred space in which an introduction to God may take place by engaging a set of issues that often hinder those who may wish to find God's presence. There are many possible spaces, but I want to pick four that, I hope, will take us into very primal places where we can wrestle as directly as possible with these core questions about how human beings come into contact with the divine. The four spaces I would like us to explore for the next chapters may be expressed in these four questions: Who is God? Why go to church? Whom can we trust? Why be moral?

Alternatively, we can express these questions as *mysteries*—meeting points between God and man: the Mystery of Jesus Christ, the Mystery of Worship, the Mystery of the Church, and the Mystery of Morality.

The purpose in asking these questions or using these titles is not to give a precise and absolute answer to any of them, but rather to sketch out a space in which we may explore, a sacred space in which we may have the possibility of being introduced to God. We will, of course, find *some* answers to these questions, but we also have to take into consideration that our answers can only ever be incomplete, because we are trying to describe realities that are beyond the limits of human thought and language. Our answers will also, of necessity, not be very thorough, as there are so many things one could say.

One last thing I would like to note here is that throughout this text, I will be quoting from a number of sources, most especially from the Bible. If you're not already a Christian, you may not accept the authority of these sources. I understand that. But perhaps you may also see the wisdom I see in them by what they actually say.

All that said, let's ask our questions and see where they may lead us. Whether we meet God there will depend greatly on ourselves.

CHAPTER TWO

The Mystery of Jesus Christ

Who Is God?

*And this is eternal life, that they may know You, the
only true God, and Jesus Christ whom You have sent.*
John 17:3

Who is God? Asking this question may seem counter-productive to our task of introduction to God. ("Why ask? Just meet Him!") There is, to be sure, some validity to that objection. We cannot really convey the truth of who God is by talking about Him. We have to get to know Him directly.

The same holds true for knowing even other human persons. Within each human person lies a mysterious well of identity that can only be met and participated in, but not satisfactorily described. So it is with God, though infinitely so, because He is infinite. The Austrian-born Jewish philosopher Martin Buber even went so far as to say that God can only ever be met in the "I-Thou" relationship, that referring to God in the grammatical third person (*He* or *Him*) makes no real sense.

Buber put it this way:

> If believing in God means being able to speak of him in the third person, then I probably do not believe in God; or at least, I do not know if it is permissible for me to say that I believe in God. For I know, when I speak of him in the third person, whenever it happens, and it has to happen again and again, there is no other way, then my tongue cleaves to the roof of my mouth so quickly that one cannot even call it speech.[3]

God is Someone we each have to meet, and any words said about Him by someone else will always fail to convey His presence fully. We may ask or answer the question, "Who is God?" but we will not actually have brought someone into contact with God by asking the question, nor by answering it. But perhaps the contemplation (even if only momentary) brought about by asking the question—and even by trying to answer it—may begin to draw a circle around the space where that contact can happen. Who is God?

That said, most of us do not have an encounter with God without first having someone ask this question for us or at least introduce us to the question. And when someone asks you that question, even just rhetorically, then you are forever prevented from considering yourself the kind of atheist who says he simply doesn't have any beliefs about the divine.

That genie cannot be put back into the bottle. The question has been asked. Our minds have begun to work on an answer. Who is God?

If we were to ask that question of the Church Fathers,‡ we might be faced with a curious answer. Many of the Fathers might first say, "There is nothing we can say about God."

This may seem counterproductive. Isn't that just giving up before we even begin? Not really. The same saints who might say that also say a lot of other things about God. But the point is that, in using human language to describe God, we are set up to fail. God is uncreated; human language is a facet of the created world. Our created language can't reliably signify uncreated reality. The sounds we make, the words we use, the sentences we put together—all of these are dependent on created reference points. We can only really talk about things we can sense, things we can conceive. But even our conceptions are created.

But God is uncreated. He is not like anything anywhere. He is not tall like my father or hard like a stone or fuzzy like a rabbit. He is not loud like a metal band or purple like a bruise or radiant like a star. Because there is such a radical disjunction between the created and the Uncreated, the creation can only tell us one thing about the Creator—that

---

‡   The term *Church Fathers* generally refers to saints and theologians through the centuries of church history who had an experience of God and taught about it clearly. Orthodox Christians consider the Church Fathers authoritative because they speak reliably from that experience.

there is one. Some folks will say they can see God in a beautiful sunset or in a majestic mountain, but everything we might say about God from such views is really just inference, usually based on our preconceptions.

We are created and He is uncreated, so we cannot comprehend Him. Even our more abstract concepts do not truly fit Him. We can say He is loving, but He is also not loving, not in the way humanity measures love. He is certainly not just according to our ideas of justice. He is also not a person in the sense that we understand personhood. He cannot be grasped, either with the hand or with the mind. He is beyond reason and even beyond theology. We therefore cannot really choose to be introduced to God or to know God. We cannot go looking for Him. Where would we even begin?

But what if He has come looking for us?

Christianity traditionally has taught that the reason we can know God is that God has revealed Himself to us as Jesus Christ. For the Orthodox, that revelation is the beginning and purpose of all theology and spiritual experience. Mankind did not find Him through reason or investigation, which is why He cannot fit into any theological or philosophical system. He is not bound by any box, even a theological box.

If you've been burned out on religion that claims to know it all, or at least seems to, then the news that God does not fit into any theological box is probably good news. (Of course, when someone tells you God doesn't fit into your box, it's usually because he doesn't like *your* box and wants you to accept *his* box instead.)

It may seem ironic for a Christian to say we cannot say anything about God. But this affirmation is our only place to make a beginning. If we are going to meet God, we have to approach the sacred meeting space with a sense that we do not own it and cannot define it. We have to sweep it clear of our preconceptions. We have to begin with a sense of wonder at the mystery, to stand awed in its presence. When we do that, then perhaps we may meet God.

This path through the unknown was essentially the approach taken in the first century by the Apostle Paul in Athens at Mars Hill (the *Areopagus*), where pagan philosophers would gather to talk. This is how he preached to these created men the uncreated God:

> "Men of Athens, I perceive that in all things you are very religious; for as I was passing through and considering the objects of your worship, I even found an altar with this inscription: TO THE UNKNOWN GOD. Therefore, the One whom you worship without knowing, Him I proclaim to you: God, who made the world and everything in it, since He is Lord of heaven and earth, does not dwell in temples made with hands. Nor is He worshiped with men's hands, as though He needed anything, since He gives to all life, breath, and all things. And He has made from one blood every nation of men to dwell on all the face of the earth, and has determined their preappointed times and the boundaries of their dwellings, so that they should seek the Lord, in the hope that they might grope for Him and find Him, though He is not far from each one of us; for in Him we live and move and have our being, as also some of your own poets have said, 'For we are also His offspring.' Therefore, since

we are the offspring of God, we ought not to think that the Divine Nature is like gold or silver or stone, something shaped by art and man's devising. Truly, these times of ignorance God overlooked, but now commands all men everywhere to repent, because He has appointed a day on which He will judge the world in righteousness by the Man whom He has ordained. He has given assurance of this to all by raising Him from the dead." (Acts 17:22–31)

In speaking to these philosophers, Paul tells them that the true God is the great unknown. Yet in the midst of this strong language about God being unknown, the apostle nevertheless says that "He is not far from each one of us; for in Him we live and move and have our being." And he tells the philosophers that, although God is unknown to them, He is making Himself known. We cannot truly seek God, though we can, in Paul's words, "grope for Him."

Yet it is God who has set out on the quest to establish contact with mankind. Christianity is not a faith of people who sat down and carefully reasoned out what God must be like. Nor is it a faith for people who want to pick up a book, even the Bible, and try to deduce what God must be or what we are supposed to do or believe. Christianity is a faith of people who stand in awe that the uncreated Creator of the universe would step into our reality and come looking for us.

We can say many things to answer this question, "Who is God?" But in the end, we have to say we don't really know. He has revealed Himself, but unless I have made the sacred space for that revelation to come to me specifically and personally, then I have no clue who God is. And even if I do get that clue, it is not something I can just hand over to someone else. Each of us has to receive that revelation for himself. The only way to open up the possibility for that revelation is to quiet ourselves and stand in wonder in that sacred space. And there, God may introduce Himself.

ETERNAL LIFE

At the heart of every human person is the desire for immortality. Some people will say they are looking forward to death, and in nonexistence they will be relieved of their suffering. But how can there be relief for someone who does not exist? There is no relief; there is just nothing. Yet implied even in that contradictory logic is the desire for immortality, the hope of something better after death.

We deeply desire to go on existing. We cannot imagine what nonexistence would be like. Try it for a moment. What if there were no you? What if the voice in your head that is you were not there? What if there were no you to be thinking these thoughts?

Most people don't think too much about death unless they are faced with their own or that of someone they love. But the truth is that each of us someday will stop breathing and die, and our bodies will grow cold. Then what? Is there life after death? Is there eternal life? Most of the world's religions teach that there is, so it would seem there is at least something in human beings that wants it.

When most of us think of eternal life, we think of it mainly in terms of perpetual existence: even though we may pass through physical death, we will continue to have being, at least in some state. Most of the world's religions believe this. It is a testament to the imprint of Himself that God put upon us that even when we are functioning with little to no direct revelation, we still believe in eternal life.

Orthodox Christianity teaches that there is, indeed, life after death. There is eternal life. But what is eternal life? It cannot mean perpetual existence in our current state, because everyone dies. But does it merely mean *existing* forever after death? Is *eternal life* just a code phrase for "going to heaven," spending life after death in a pleasant place instead of what Shakespeare's Hamlet so glibly calls "the other place"?

Christians believe that God's revelation to us is centered in His Son, incarnate as the God-man Jesus Christ. So what does Jesus have to say about the nature of eternal life?

In His great high-priestly prayer to God the Father, shortly before His crucifixion and death, Jesus says this: "Father, the hour has come. Glorify Your Son, that Your Son also may glorify You, as You have given Him authority over all flesh, that He should give eternal life to as many as You have given Him. And this is eternal life, that they may know You, the only true God, and Jesus Christ whom You have sent" (John 17:1–3). We read here that it is from Jesus that we can receive eternal life. But listen closely to how He defines it: "this is eternal life, that they may know You, the only true God, and Jesus Christ whom You have sent."

This definition of eternal life cuts right through much of the pointless religious garbage that often passes for Christianity. Jesus does not say the purpose of our faith is to make us "good people" or that it's about "going to heaven" when we die. Nor is Christianity about feeling good, meeting religious people, knowing about theology, etc. Eternal life is to know God the Father and to know Jesus Christ, whom He sent. Though He doesn't say it here, it is implied that it is to know the Holy Spirit as well, since in Christian theology the Spirit is one with the Father and Son, and since, as Paul tells us in 1 Corinthians 12:3, no one can say that Jesus is Lord (i.e., know that He is God) except by the Holy Spirit. That's what it means to have eternal life—knowing God—so we have to get it right.

This definition might strike us as simplistic. Of course we want to know God. But do we? Are we prepared for an encounter with the almighty, uncreated Father, Son, and Holy Spirit? Even Christians' thoughts and actions often reveal that we are fine with knowing church services, with knowing theology, with knowing other religious people— but, well, *knowing God*, now, that's another matter. That's dangerous, because God is not tamable. He is not predictable. He is not bound by our expectations, concepts, or preferences. He does not have to come when we call. But that's eternal life according to Jesus—it's knowing God.

Even those whose image of eternal life is defined by "going to heaven" know this at least implicitly. It's not as if we could go to heaven and not run into God while we were there. And like the people whom C. S. Lewis writes about in his novel *The Great Divorce* (in which a tour bus provides rides from hell to heaven), we will experience the awful, terrifying reality of heaven in one of two ways: as strong people who were prepared for that much truth and beauty and absolutely love it; or as delusional people who live lives of such illusion and unreality that heaven's very realness will be painful and horrible. In Lewis's novel, everyone is allowed to get out of the bus and stay if they like, but heaven is just too much for the people from hell, so they choose to go back.

And we may remember another image of the encounter with God that Lewis uses, this time in his *Chronicles of Narnia*. In those books, Jesus Christ is depicted symbolically as a lion called Aslan. He is at once terrifying, glorious, loving, good, wise, delightful, and playful. But it is often said in those books that he is "not a tame lion."

Eternal life is knowing and becoming one with Jesus Christ, the Lion of Judah (an ancient prophetic name for Jesus), who cannot be held down, defined, or bargained with. And like Lewis's Aslan in the first of the Narnia books, He's coming back, and when He does, everyone will have to answer for how he's lived his life. If you find this even slightly frightening, then you are beginning to know what it means to have the fear of God.

But the fear of God is the beginning of knowledge (Prov. 1:7), and that knowledge eventually leads us not to terror, but to reverence. And so it is with this fear, this deep reverence and awe for the ineffable immensity of our God, that we proceed with knowing Him.

THE EPISTEMOLOGY OF DOXOLOGY

Since mankind first received the revelation of God, his initial reaction has been fear, especially after the Fall from grace Adam and Eve committed in the Garden of Eden. We read in Genesis (the first book of the Bible) how, after Adam and Eve sinned, they hid themselves from God out of fear, but God came looking for them.

The narrative of Adam and Eve gets repeated for all of us. Because of our imperfection and the evil that resides in our hearts, when God comes looking for us—if we permit the encounter—our reaction may be fear. We can imagine that the Apostle Paul, when he was struck down by a blinding light and heard the voice of Christ on the road to Damascus, was struck with fear, because he learned at that moment that the Church he (as Saul) had been persecuting was the Church God Himself had established (Acts 9:1–5).

This experience brings us to the great question of epistemology—a philosophical term for the method by which we know anything. Following Jesus' definition of eternal life, what we wish to know is God, because we wish to have eternal life. But if the fear of God is the beginning of knowledge, then does that mean we are to live as petrified people, perpetually frightened, in order to be true believers? No, for the fear of God is only the *beginning* of knowledge. Where this takes us is not to an epistemology of "theophobia"— being afraid of God. Rather, we are brought to an epistemology of *doxology,* or praise. That is, the only way to know God is to praise Him.

Why is this the only way to know God? For one thing, we are not reverencing God if we are not inspired to praise Him. Anyone who encounters God and does not praise Him is either not truly encountering Him or does not truly fear and reverence Him. And if we do not fear and reverence Him, then we cannot know Him.

Even to the secular mind, this should make some sense, because it is only in humility that we are capable of gaining any knowledge. We must realize we do not know everything. Within this realization is the possibility of wonder at the encounter with the unknown. And if a person with humility wonders at the majesty of God, then he will want to glorify Him, and the doxological purpose of man's being is revealed (*doxology* means "word of glory," i.e., praise).

We are creatures that want to worship, though we often worship the wrong thing. But if we can turn that basic power of our human nature in the right direction, toward God, then we will find ourselves worshiping Him.

Beyond being inspired by God's awesomeness when we experience Him, there is something else about doxology that grants knowledge of God, and it is at the heart of traditional Christian worship itself. In the modern forms of worship of many Christians, God is certainly praised. But it is only within traditional, sacramental Christianity that worship is understood as *uniting* the worshiper to the One being worshiped. And in that union comes mystical, experiential, transformative knowledge. This knowledge is beyond the wisdom gained from living an ethical life and instead is more personal, direct, and intimate. Orthodox Christianity is thus not reducible to an ethical system wherein we merely learn how to behave correctly. Rather, it is a faith whose purpose is deeply knowing God—the vision of Christ in glory.

Worship is the primary means by which we know God, and worship (as we will see in the next chapter) has a particular form in Christianity that is authentic. But if we try to know God through means we devise for ourselves, then we are denying ourselves the actual tools for the job. It would be like trying to see microscopic life without a microscope. We cannot know God without authentically worshiping Him, and thus we cannot have eternal life without worshiping Him.

But what makes this mystical union even possible? How can we who are so different from and so separated from God become one with Him?

THE INCARNATION

Some theologians of the Orthodox Church suggest that God would have become man even if Adam and Eve had not fallen from grace, that the Incarnation of the Son of God was presupposed in the creation. Christians conceive of the Incarnation of the Son of God primarily in terms of Jesus' mission to rescue mankind from sin, corruption, and death. Yet even if the Fall had not occurred, it is still part of our nature to be radically different from God. He created us this way. Now, you might object, if you have read the book of Genesis, that man is made according to God's image, and you would be correct. So, if we were made according to His image, how were we created as separated from Him?

Let's think of this in terms perhaps a little more familiar to us. You can see an artist dimly in the images he creates, drawing conclusions about who he must be, but his creations live on without him and have an existence apart from him. They do not depend on him for continued existence, nor can we say they are united to him. This, sadly, is the way many people see God: He created everything in six days, rested on the seventh day, then immediately went into retirement and hasn't been heard from since. This position is properly called *deism*. Even if they do not explicitly believe that way, many Christians act as if they believed that God is not really present or interested in us.

But we were made according to the image of God. Some

translations of Genesis say we are made "in" His image, but
the Old Testament Scriptures used by the Orthodox Church
(the Septuagint) use a more precise phrase, that we are made
"according to" His image (Gen. 1:26). But what is the image
of God? According to *what*, exactly, are we made?

We are made according to Jesus Christ, who in Colossians
1:15 is called "the image of the invisible God." Christ is our
template. When we were made, the Holy Trinity had Christ
in mind, because He is the image of God. Christ was the
model, the template from which the divine Artist painted
us, the stamp from which we are stamped. Indeed, Colossians 1:15 even goes so far as to describe Christ paradoxically
as "the firstborn over all creation."

Therefore, in that sense we may say that the Incarnation
was presupposed from the beginning of creation. Our nature
when it is alone is radically different from and separated from
God, but our nature was never created to exist by itself. We
were instead designed for communion with God in Christ.
In scientific terms, human beings were not designed to be
"closed systems." We were designed for interaction with our
Creator, to incorporate His activity, which gets cut off from
us when we sin. This is why we are described in Ephesians 2:1
as being "dead" when we are in "trespasses and sins."

To many people today, the unbelievable claim of the
Incarnation is supposedly that this man Jesus claims to be
God. But we should remember that this kind of skepticism
is not what greeted the doctrine when it was first preached

by the apostles. At that time, the skepticism went the other way. People could accept that He was God, but it seemed ridiculous to say that God had become a man—not just that he *appeared* to be a man, but that a divine person had actually taken on true humanity. The ancient world knew that divinity was "out there," but it found the claim absurd when the apostles preached that God had come and dwelt among us as one of us.

So what does the Incarnation mean? What exactly is this crazy, absurd, revolutionary claim the first Christians made that the Greco-Roman world found so incredible?

In the simplest terms, the Incarnation means that the Second Person of the Holy Trinity, the Son of God who is fully God, without setting aside any part of what it means to be God, became a real, flesh-and-blood human being. The word *incarnation* literally means "enfleshment." *Incarnation* is related to words like *carnivorous* and *carnal* and even the *carne* of *chili con carne*. It all refers to "flesh," most literally, to "meat." If we were to say that the Son of God took on "meat," then we might begin to understand the way those first-century pagans felt when they were told that God became man. It sounds absurd, even irreverent, to speak in that way. God surely would not become meat!

Yet this is exactly what we're saying. The invisible, ineffable, incomprehensible God took on real, fleshy, meaty, solid, bodily existence. Perhaps we should use high-and-mighty words like *flesh* a little less when talking about this, and use words like *meat, skin, bones, hair,* and maybe even *eyeballs.* These are all good words that get us thinking about the human body in all its solidity and limitations. This is what happened when the Son of God was conceived miraculously in the womb of the Virgin Mary. He took on all that stuff.

Besides the meaty, material meaning behind the word *incarnation,* Jesus' human existence also includes all the immateriality of what it means to be human. He has a human soul. He has a human mind. He has a human will. He did not animate a body with some otherworldly force, like a zombie. No, that human body is *His* human body, and it is animated by *His* human soul.

The Incarnation is such a central doctrine to the Christian faith that it has remained the subject of debate for centuries. Numerous heretics (people who, given the choice, choose something other than the Orthodox faith they formerly believed) have attempted to chip away at the experience of the Church. First, they said He only appeared to be human. Next, they said He was some sort of divine creature, but still just a creature and not the Creator. Next, they said His mother only gave birth to a human nature, that the God part somehow got inserted later. Then, they said He didn't have a human soul or mind. Next, they said His divine nature swallowed up His human nature. Then, they said He had only a divine will and not a human will. Later, they said He only had divine energies and not human energies. ("Energies" are the presence and working of a person in the world.)

And then they said it was not proper to depict His humanity in images. It seemed heretics would say almost anything to knock holes in this reality—that a single Person is both God and man simultaneously, in every way that could mean.

But the Orthodox Church still teaches the same thing: Jesus Christ is God, and He is man, complete and perfect in both. He is one Person in two natures. We call this the *hypostatic union*: in one hypostasis ("person" or "concrete entity") there are two natures. Christ is the only hypostatic union there is. Everything else, whether created or uncreated, has only one nature—even the other two Persons of the Trinity (the Father and the Holy Spirit), and even the various hypostases of nature, such as animals, plants, rocks, etc.

This is the mystery of Jesus Christ, that in Him are united the heavenly and the earthly, the divine and the human, the celestial and the terrestrial, the created and the Uncreated. We cannot understand what this truly means. All we know is what He has revealed to us, and all of the Orthodox Church's doctrine, all its theology, all its worship, all its religious activity are attempts to live in and explore that revelation. Even our dogma, which uses very precise language, can only draw *boundaries* around the faith in order to protect it from heretical attacks. It says very little about what's inside those boundaries. Even the content of the Gospel story itself does not openly display the inner reality.

For the Orthodox, dogma isn't about being closed-minded and nasty. Rather, dogmas are those truths we hold fast to without compromise, because they are what has been revealed by God. They're not anyone's personal opinions. No mere opinion is worth that level of commitment.

So now that we've said something about what the Incarnation is, we should open up its purpose a little. We said earlier that mankind was not meant to live an isolated existence, apart from the ongoing, life-giving involvement of God. So we need access to God. But because we are created beings, there is no place in creation through which we can make the connection to the uncreated God. That is why the Son of God becomes the Son of Mary, the Son of Man. Because He is now human, we can access His humanity, which is created as we are. We can touch it. And in touching His humanity, we access His divinity.

We call this a "mystery," because, even while it was revealed that God became man, we do not really know *how* this could have happened. Even the Virgin Mary in all her holiness found it incredible when the Archangel Gabriel told her about this at the Annunciation. The saints do not claim to understand it, and the angels themselves stand amazed at it. Wonder is at the heart of our encounter with Christ, and it is even expressed iconographically in the architecture of Orthodox churches: Behind and above the altar in many churches is an icon of the Virgin Mary with Christ in her womb, and the caption reads "more spacious than the heavens"—that is, her womb must somehow be more spacious than the heavens themselves, which cannot contain God, to have the God-man dwelling within it. When we encounter Christ, we encounter the great mystery of the universe—the God who is man, the man who is God.

Here is the point at which Orthodox Christianity parts ways with rationalism, because no matter how hard we try, no matter how much we speculate, no matter how smart we are, we cannot *define* the God who dwelt in a human womb and took flesh from that mother. And here also is the point at which we part ways from certain kinds of Far Eastern mysticism, because our purpose is not to escape from the world of the physical into the world of the divine. We do not seek to be absorbed into God. No, we as distinct, discrete persons are encountering the pinnacle of personhood, the Second Person of the Trinity, Jesus Christ, and in Him, we also encounter the Father and the Spirit, and we get there through the physical reality of the Incarnation.

When people run into Jesus in the Gospels (those Bible books that record His life), we see a variety of results. Some ignored Him. Some ridiculed Him. Some wanted to hear more. Some went away sad or confused or angry. Some plotted against Him. Some crucified Him. But some believed. And all were changed. It is because an encounter with the God-man Jesus Christ reveals us for who we truly are, which is then magnified. We are either inspired to repentance and holiness, or we react by becoming darkened and calcified, confirmed in our hardness of heart.

And this encounter need not be a one-time event, either. It

may be the initial conversion, or it may be the ongoing call to repent, to grow in faith and love. Whatever happens, when we come into contact with Christ, we will either become more like Him or less like Him. We can take the encounter and use it to turn toward or away from Christ. This is why the preaching of the Gospel constitutes the Church—because of the response to its power, because it provides an encounter with Christ. And that is the Gospel.

Gospel is a native English word coming from our ancient English heritage, from the period scholars call Anglo-Saxon or Old English. *Gospel* comes from *Godspell*, the "good spell." We now think of this as "good news," but this word *spell* still suggests power, such as in the phrases *magic spell* or *that spells trouble*. The Gospel is a good word that has power to it. And Jesus Christ is called the *Word* of God (John 1)—the One who is the messenger and the content of the message.

ENCOUNTERING THE MYSTERY

So what is this powerful message? The Gospel consists of these three affirmations: Jesus Christ is the Messiah. He rose from the dead. Humanity can therefore be saved.

First, what does it mean that Jesus is the Messiah? Historically, this identifies Him as the hoped-for Savior of the people of ancient Israel, the "anointed one" of God. (The Hebrew-derived *Messiah* means "anointed one," and so does the Greek-derived *Christ*.) *Messiah* is a word rich with meaning for the ancient Jews, and Jesus is the One who bears all that meaning in Himself. He comes to rescue His people Israel from their separation from God, to save them from the sins that have made that separation happen. And He also comes to redefine Israel, because the encounter with the Christ leaves nothing and no one unchanged, even whole nations. Since the coming of Christ, Israel is now composed not of an ethnic identification, but of the people who have believed in Him and live in Him—the Church, the New Israel. Affirming that He is the Messiah also puts Jesus into history, which could not have God in it if He had not become incarnate. To call Him *Messiah* is to believe in His incarnation as a real man who lived and moved in real history. And history, having encountered the Messiah, has never been the same.

Secondly, the Orthodox Christian greeting "Christ is risen!"—with which we celebrate the great Feast of Feasts, Holy Pascha, Christ's resurrection, for the forty days until His Ascension—is a critical element of the Gospel message. If Christ is not risen, then the preaching of the apostles is pointless, and so is the faith of those who believe them (1 Cor. 15:14). The New Testament affirms that, after Christ truly died on the cross, He conquered the power of death by bringing His divinity into contact with death by means of His humanity. For while God is undying, the God become man could indeed die. And we find in the same pages of the New Testament both the affirmation that God raised Christ from the dead (Rom. 8:11) and that Christ raised Himself from the dead (John 2:19). Taken together, these two affirmations show that Christ is God, for if God raised Him from the dead, and if He raised Himself from the dead, then He must be God. To say that He is risen is to affirm both His deity, in that He could do such a thing, and His humanity, for if He were not human, He could not have died. It is once again to believe in and put our trust in the Incarnation, that Christ is the God-man.

Finally, the Gospel message is that humanity may be saved as a result of Jesus' being the Messiah and His resurrection from the dead. It is because we can touch and connect with His humanity that we can partake of His divinity (2 Pet. 1:4). It is by participating in His life that we receive His transformation of our own lives. By connecting with Him, we can live with His righteousness, which is not just moral living but living by the potential we were created for. By connecting with Him, we can gradually acquire His wisdom and power. By connecting with Him, our own deaths can also trample down the power of death and find their fulfillment in resurrection. What we are saved *from* is corruption and death.

That is the Gospel, that we can become by grace what He is by His nature. We cannot become identical with the one, Almighty God, but we can become filled up and united with the divine presence. Jesus Christ is God present as a man, and we can become men and women who show forth the presence of God.

As we conclude this chapter, let me once again reaffirm that we really do not know what we're talking about. Yes, we have said many things that touch upon what God has revealed to us about Himself, and we could speak for years, and even then, we would only just begin to pass somewhere by the reality of the divine. There is no word that can contain God, even though there was, somehow, a womb that contained the Uncontainable.

And within that womb was not just a new life, but the Life, the Life-giver Himself, the One who invented life and who sustains it, the One who offers eternal life to all who are daring enough to go take it, to those who are willing to take the Kingdom of Heaven by "violence": "the kingdom of heaven suffers violence, and the violent take it by force" (Matt. 11:12).

And what is that eternal life? It is to know Him, to know that uncontainable, invisible, ineffable, perfect, infinite, uncreated God who was contained, who became visible, who can be grasped with the mind (though just barely), who suffered the effects of imperfection yet without sinning, who became finite and created. Eternal life is to know the God of us all, the Lord who loves us and saves us, even while we run away from Him. This is the great mystery of the Incarnation, the mystery of Jesus Christ, the Gospel message, the good word that has the power to transform us.

And in hearing that word and responding in faith, we come to know the Holy Trinity, the one God. We could spend many more pages discussing the Orthodox doctrine of the Trinity, but that would be beyond the scope of this work. But know, at least, that everything begins with Christ, and in Him, we receive the life of the Holy Trinity, the Father, the Son, and the Holy Spirit, three divine Persons in one essence, whose uncreated energies—His grace—pervade all of creation and make our union with Him possible. Our knowledge of the Holy Trinity comes only in and through Christ.

We said earlier that the only way to know this God who stepped into history through the Incarnation is to praise Him, to worship Him, to give Him glory, and thus be mystically united to Him. I will therefore conclude this chapter by quoting from an anonymous Christian poem of praise written around AD 800, penned originally in Old English. Two lines from this poem inspired the great twentieth-century writer J. R. R. Tolkien, an ardent Christian, who, when he read these lines, heard within them the beginning of a new world, one he called "Middle-earth." These lines as he read them looked like this: *Eala earendel, engla beorhtast, / ofer middangeard monnum sended.* Literally, they mean "Hail, Day-star, brightest angel, over Middle-earth sent to men" (*middangeard* is also sometimes rendered "throughout the earth").

This passage, which begins with those lines that inspired Tolkien so brilliantly to teach us through his fiction about human nature and the war between good and evil, also may be seen to summarize everything we have tried to say in this chapter. Here is the whole of that passage, fully translated into Modern English, from the poem entitled simply "Christ":

Hail, Day-star! Brightest angel sent to man throughout the earth, and Thou steadfast splendor of the sun, bright above stars! Ever Thou dost illumine with Thy light the time of every season. As Thou, begotten God of God, Son of the true Father, without beginning abodest ever in the splendour of heaven, so now for need Thy handiwork beseecheth boldly that Thou send the bright sun unto us; that Thou come and shed Thy light on those who long ere this, compassed about with mist and in the darkness, clothed in sin, sit here in the long night, and must needs endure the dark shadow of Death. Now are we full of hope and put our trust in Thy salvation, heralded to the hosts of men by the Word of God, which in the beginning was with God, with the Almighty Father coeternal, and afterward was made flesh unstained of sin, which the Virgin bare, a solace unto wretched men. God was seen among us without sin; together dwelt the mighty Son of God and the son of man, in peace among the people. Wherefore, we may rightfully give thanks forever to our Victor-Lord, that He would send Himself to us. [4]

CHAPTER THREE

The Mystery of Worship
Why Go to Church?

*O Lord God Almighty, who alone art holy, who dost
accept a sacrifice of praise from those who call upon
Thee with their whole heart: Receive also the prayer of
us sinners, and lead us to Thy holy altar, and enable
us to offer unto Thee gifts and spiritual sacrifices for
our sins and for the ignorance of the people, and make
us worthy to find grace in Thy sight, that our sacrifice
may be acceptable unto Thee and that the good Spirit
of Thy grace may rest upon us, and upon these gifts
here spread forth, and upon all Thy people.*
—Prayer of the Proskomedia,
Divine Liturgy of St. John Chrysostom

Why go to church? People may give various answers to
this question:

» I like being there.
» Someone expects me to be there.

» I meet my friends or my family there.

» I feel inspired when I go there.

People also give various reasons not to go to church:

» I don't like it there.

» I can pray on my own better outside of church.

» I want to sleep in.

» I'm busy.

But none of those answers addresses the real reason to go to church, the reason we need to go to church. The Orthodox Church's teachings could be described with this answer: *We are born thirsty.*

Anyone who has ever been around a newborn baby, especially mothers, knows this. This thirst is unmistakable in a purely physical sense, in that we are always in need of drink, but it is even more urgent in a spiritual sense. We are always in need of divine drink. Without this supply of life from the divine Source, we go thirsty. We may be able to function for a while without drinking from the Source, but eventually we grow weak and incapable of spiritual activity. Whether we are even aware of who we really are in physical or spiritual terms, the truth is that we are not complete in ourselves. We have need of infinity, of inexhaustible completeness, in order to keep ourselves whole.

God made us this way. Some may argue that was a cruel thing to do, to create us so that we are lacking something, so we do not inherently have immortality without contribution from an outside source. But this argument either betrays an ignorance of the joy we can obtain from a proper under-standing of what it means to be human, or it represents a very dark and sinister vision of our humanity.

Let's think about this: If we wish God had made us self-sustaining, whole in ourselves, without the great thirst, we are wishing to be utterly and wholly alone. The only possible ethic to be built on a sense of exclusive personal being is an antisocial one. All the things human beings see worth in—love, compassion, hope, faith, kindness, self-sacrifice, heroism—only make sense if practiced in the context of relationship. These noble virtues all presume a human person stepping outside himself in order to believe in, act toward, and connect with those outside himself. A human person without the great thirst is a person unconcerned, isolated, divided, and deeply selfish.

Our incompleteness is therefore a blessing from God. But even if we do not believe that, it is nevertheless the way we are made. Even before Adam and Eve's sin, which distorted human life, God made us to have a desire to connect with Him and with each other. The thirst for communion is not the imposition of a God who cannot bear to have other self-sufficient beings in His universe. Rather, this design for mankind is exactly what reveals to us the divine stamp on mankind, that we are made according to His image. God is Father, Son, and Holy Spirit, three Persons having one Being, the Holy Trinity. The very nature of God is to be in communion. We resemble His Trinitarian life in that we too have our fullness in communion. And the truest way we can have communion with God is in worship.

WHAT IS WORSHIP?

The great thirst for communion is the ground on which the worship of God happens, and therefore it is why we need to go to church, which is where worship happens in its fullness. We'll get to what that means later, but first we should ask what worship is.

Some folks think worship is simply one being bowing down to another, perhaps saying how great that other being is while doing the bowing down. Such people identify worship with subservience, obeisance, groveling, etc. Of course, there is a certain truth to this definition, that worship involves giving respect and honor to the other, humbling oneself before the other. The word *worship* in English comes from the word *worth*, and in its most basic sense, to worship another is to demonstrate the worthiness of the other.

Even the two Greek words that sometimes get translated as "worship"—*proskeunesis* and *latreia*—literally mean "kissing toward" and "serving," respectively. Over the course of church history, those words came to have distinct technical meanings: proskeunesis is the veneration given to holy persons, objects, and places, while latreia is the worship, service, and adoration due to God alone. The word *idolatry* includes latreia, and it literally means "serving a fantasy."

But Orthodox Christian worship of the Holy Trinity consists not merely of the outwardly visible acts of kissing, bowing, singing words of respect and reverence, and so forth. Yes, these are some of the things we do when we worship God, but there is also something happening within. When we perform these outward acts toward God, and when they are done with the right inner attitude, it is worship.

So what happens when we do these things? What does our giving worship to God have to do with the great thirst we have for Him?

From a skeptical, secular point of view, the worship of God has little to do with our need for communion with Him. After all, how does bowing down before someone and saying how great he is fulfill any need for communion? At best, this communion must only be virtual—that is, it resembles communion and even has some effects that imitate communion, but it is not communion. It has to be fantasy, right?

We can see this clearly in the many modern idolatries that surround us. There is a great cult of celebrity in our society. There are also cults of politics, food, the body, sex, and money. In all these pursuits, people are literally engaging in idolatry—they are serving *fantasy*. In worshiping a celebrity, we do not actually know him. But we imagine ourselves to be identified with him in some way. We may even try to look like him. In worshiping politics and ideology, we may be worshiping politicians as celebrities, but we may also be worshiping ideologies, believing that we somehow become better people by being positioned within the correct political camp. In pursuing the cult of food or any other bodily aspect such as sexuality, we are following after a phantom image, in which we present a "taste" or a "look" to the world and to ourselves, hoping that those things will define us, will fill us up, perhaps even literally.

Whether we are filling up our bellies or transgressing against our flesh or attempting to possess the flesh of another through lust, we are pursuing phantoms that will never satisfy and will always demand more. The same is true of money, as well, which is getting more fantastical all the time, since our currencies are not backed by anything other than someone's word.

It is no wonder that all these worldly pursuits are so conducive to addiction. Addiction is the increasing need for something that cannot satisfy, cannot complete the human person. And so we serve the fantasy even more.

But true worship of God has a different effect. While the addiction born out of idolatry leads to erratic, insane, destructive behaviors, proper worship of the Holy Trinity leads instead to peace, to wholeness, to sanity, to creativity. Why is this? Why is it that when we turn our worship to created things, we do not slake the great thirst, but find ourselves even more thirsty? And why is it that when we turn our worship to the *uncreated* Being—that is, to God—we find that we are satisfied and whole?

In its most basic sense, it is due to the nature of the

source. Created things are by nature corruptible and finite. This finiteness is worsened by the Fall of mankind, which brought all of created nature with it. But the uncreated Being is incorruptible and infinite. Therefore, when we drink from a finite source, we find that it will run out. But the infinite Source never runs out. Likewise, when we drink from a corruptible source, we receive corruption, the tendency for everything to break down—in physics terms, this is entropy. But when we drink from the incorruptible Source, we receive incorruption, which grants healing, wholeness, and energy. In other terms, you cannot clean with dirty water, and you cannot fix with a broken tool. But when you use pure water or a working tool, you can accomplish something.

But such purely functional language regarding worship does not get at its inner reality. In worship, we become joined to the other, and in that joining, we *become* the other. This becoming is never a total re-identification. I cannot turn into a celebrity by worshiping him. I cannot turn into food or money by worshiping it. But I nevertheless become transformed by those images, corruptible and finite as they are, because we as changeable human persons are deeply affected by whatever and whomever we give ourselves over to. Just as hanging with the wrong crowd changes you to be like them, worshiping idols, which are delusions, makes you like them.

In worshiping *God*, however, to use the words of the fourth-century saint Athanasius the Great, we can "become god." Whether you want to spell *god* there with a big "G" or a little "g," Athanasius does not mean that we turn into the Almighty God, nor into petty deities such as the ancient pagans worshiped; but we are nevertheless transformed by the encounter in worship. We take on the attributes of the One we worship. We share a union without fusion, a communion in which the persons remain distinct but come to be one with each other. True worship grants an intimacy beyond emotion, beyond respect, beyond intellectual knowledge.

Worship therefore is not just a matter of honoring another, or even of bowing down and serving another. That is properly called *veneration*, and it is proper to venerate persons and objects worthy of it. To *worship*, however, is to give oneself over to the other. This act includes bowing down and serving, but at a deeper level, it is to join oneself to the other. It is communion.

THE CENTER OF WORSHIP:
THE EUCHARIST

Because worship of God is communion, a direct connection and union of the human person with the divine Persons, the content of worship is not only words or outward actions. It is not enough merely to tell God that He is great, powerful, magnificent, and so forth. It is not enough merely to teach about God—which isn't even veneration, much less worship.

It is also not enough to feel good feelings toward God. All of that can be done from home or out in the woods.

Some people describe themselves as "spiritual but not religious." They say they commune with God out in a beautiful forest far better than they can in church. They may even call what they're doing *worship*, a word that now gets used for nearly any kind of religious activity. But *how* is this person worshiping God? Is that really worship?

Ancient pagans knew exactly how they worshiped their gods. They put animals on altars, killed them, and then burned them. The Jews did the same thing. Throughout the history of the world, worship in nearly every religion has involved sacrifice, surrounded with incense, religious imagery, and so forth. That worship must be *physical* is one of the most basic intuitions of mankind, even outside of the divine revelation begun with the Jews and completed in the Church. Both within and outside that revelation, ancient worship was earthy and bloody. In the history of human worship, there is a focus on materiality, and most especially on blood.

There's just something about blood. The ancient world had a fascination with blood. Followers of the Mithraist pagan mystery cult in the Roman Empire would ritually bathe themselves in the blood of bulls, believing that doing so would grant them immortality.

Worship of the *true* God has always been about blood, too, even since the days of Cain and Abel, the sons of Adam and Eve. When Noah and his family were saved in the ark, he offered a blood sacrifice to God. When God saved Isaac, his father Abraham offered a blood sacrifice to God. When Moses led the Hebrews out of Egypt, God instituted for Aaron and his descendants in the priesthood a complex system of blood sacrifices as the worship of Israel. The priests of the Old Covenant offered up bulls, goats, and sheep on the altar, first in the mobile tabernacle and then later in the permanent temple. (Much of this is described in detail in the Old Testament Book of Leviticus.) Worship has always involved blood.

In the extended meditation on the priesthood that is the Epistle to the Hebrews, it thus makes complete sense for the Apostle Paul, in writing to Jewish people, to make use of the image of blood when talking about the priesthood of Christ (Heb. 9:11-14). The underlying message of the whole epistle is that the priesthood of the Old Covenant has now been fulfilled by the priesthood of Christ. And in the ninth chapter of Hebrews, Christ's priesthood is talked about specifically in terms of blood. Indeed, blood is mentioned twenty-two different times in this epistle, out of hundreds of references to it throughout the Bible.

What is all this about blood? Why do we see this theme repeated not only in the Jewish and then Christian Scriptures, but in nearly every culture and religion in human history, both for believers and unbelievers? Why do our minds always get back to blood?

The key is to be found in the book we referenced earlier, Leviticus, whose primary character is that of a liturgical guide to worship. Leviticus directs the Jewish people of the tribe of Levi, who were appointed by God to be the priestly tribe, how to lead the worship of Israel. It is an extremely detailed book, just like the liturgical books used in the Orthodox Church.

In Leviticus 17:11, we read the key to this whole question of blood: "For the life of the flesh is in the blood, and I have given it to you upon the altar to make atonement for your souls, for it is the blood that makes atonement for the soul." The context of this verse is God forbidding the Jews to drink the blood of animals, but He makes this prohibition by way of telling them what blood is and what it's for. Blood is where we find life, and blood is for making atonement for the soul.

How is this possible? It is because in order for us to connect to something, to commune with it, we have to meet with the same type of thing that we are. That is, because we are creatures, we cannot connect directly with the uncreated Being except through created being. We cannot access the heavenly except through the earthly.

We may be tempted to think this means that life has to be taken, that there must be death, in order for sins to be forgiven. Indeed, this is how many people interpret the death of Jesus, that God wanted Him killed in order to appease His wrath against mankind. But this misses the whole point of what atonement means. It is not so much about doing away with criminal charges related to God's law, but rather about union and communion with God.

In ancient Jewish worship and even in much pagan worship, the blood of sacrificed animals was not merely offered up on the altar. Rather, the blood was sprinkled or poured out on places and, most especially, on people. That is, the life that was being poured out to bring about forgiveness, long life, or immortality was being identified with the people making the sacrifice. They were receiving the life of that animal onto themselves.

And were they merely getting bloody? No, this blood had been sacrificed, which means that it had been offered up to be made holy. The word *sacrifice* is intimately connected with other words like *sacred, sanctify, sacrament,* and the Latin word *sacerdos,* which means "priest." Thus, this animal blood was being put on the altar, it received holiness from a divine source, and then that holy blood was put on the worshiper.

It is in *that* liturgical context that Jesus Christ comes into the world. And the Epistle to the Hebrews asks us: If the blood of these animals purified the flesh of worshipers in the Jewish tabernacle and temple, then how much more so will the blood of Jesus—that is, the blood of God—purify the very souls of mankind?

But the point goes even deeper when we consider Christian worship, which is the fulfillment of all the religious and even non-religious hopes that have, for so many thousands of years, focused on blood. While Jews and pagans were sprinkled with blood or sometimes ashes from the sacrifice in order to have their sins forgiven or their lives bettered, Christians are not merely sprinkled with animal blood. No, they *eat and drink* the very Body and Blood of their Creator become a Man.

Now, lest we be tempted to think that eating and drinking Christ's Body and Blood is only meant to be a metaphor, it may be helpful to know that early Christians took this so seriously that one of the common accusations from the surrounding pagan culture was that Christians were cannibals!

Likewise, in John 6, Jesus says this: "Most assuredly, I say to you, unless you eat the flesh of the Son of Man and drink His blood, you have no life in you. Whoever eats My flesh and drinks My blood has eternal life, and I will raise him up at the last day. For My flesh is food indeed, and My blood is drink indeed. He who eats my flesh and drinks My blood abides in Me, and I in him" (John 6:53–56). Some of Christ's followers heard that and turned away from Him. He didn't call them back, reassuring them that it was just a metaphor (John 6:66). He was serious.

There's nothing wrong with loving nature (indeed, it can teach us to love God), but taking a walk in the woods doesn't get you access to the Eucharist. Orthodox Christians also find God out in the beauty of the created world, but God did not become incarnate as a tree or a mountain lake. While the heavens and the earth and all created things do indeed declare the glory of God and draw our attention to Him, they do not give us access to commune with Him in true worship. He became incarnate as a human man, and thus the only complete, fulfilled way to commune with Him is through the flesh and blood He makes available to us as the Eucharist.

WORSHIP IN THE BIBLE

If we think seriously about the Eucharist, we will realize that it implies a great many things. For one thing, it means our worship of God is not conducted according to our own design. Because God has an objective, independent existence apart from any of our ideas about Him or our preferences for how we want Him to operate, we must connect to Him in worship on His terms, not on ours. This truth is also the reason the walker in the woods is not really worshiping God there. From the Christian point of view, truth is something that is revealed by God, not something we derive out of our feelings about who He might be. And in the revelation of God, first to the Jews and then to the Church, nothing is said about worshiping God with a disincarnate, walk-in-the-woods approach. Again, walking in the woods and even having a spiritual experience there can be powerful, but that's not the same thing as worship.

There is real, particular solidity to worshiping God properly. Why? Why can we not just decide for ourselves how we want to worship God? Isn't it the thought that counts? Isn't the particular style of worship just a matter of taste? Does God really care about the details? Christian history shows that there has been a striking unanimity down through the centuries when it comes to worshiping God, so how one does it is clearly important for Christians. To understand that unanimity, let's take a quick look at the history of worship in the Bible.

The first time worship is mentioned in the Bible is in Genesis 4, in the context of the second great sin in the history of mankind—the first murder, when the firstborn son of Adam and Eve, Cain, kills his brother Abel. In that account, Abel brings to God a sacrifice from his flock of sheep, and Cain brings a sacrifice of vegetables. We don't know that God has given them specific, detailed instructions for worship yet (though He certainly does later, in the Book of Leviticus), but we do know that He rejects Cain's offering while accepting Abel's. Why does God reject Cain's offering? St. Cyprian of Carthage, a third-century North African bishop, tells us, "God looked, not at their gifts, but at their hearts, and the gift He accepted came from the heart that pleased Him."[5]

Now, we may be tempted to look at this quote from Cyprian and think it justifies a free-for-all approach to worship—as long as one's heart is in the right place, what do the details of worship matter? But we should also consider that, while what made Cain and Abel's sacrifices *different* was the state of their hearts, the two also had something *in common*: they were both physical sacrifices of physical objects, offered up to God. The sacrifice God accepted was not one from someone who wanted a disincarnate worship experience but rather from Abel, a shepherd, who offered up his sheep to God. This same pattern continues throughout the Old Testament, with animal sacrifices being the standard for people like Noah, Abraham, Aaron, the kings of Israel, and so on. And of course, the Book of Leviticus is essentially a liturgical manual, giving extremely detailed instructions directly from God to the ancient Jews as to how He is to be worshiped.

Besides including liturgical instructions, Leviticus also includes some narrative that bears directly on its liturgical contents. We remember that the first priest God ordained for the people of Israel was Moses' brother Aaron. Along with Aaron, the whole tribe of Levi (for whom Leviticus is named) was designated as the priestly tribe. Thus, it was appropriate that Aaron's two sons, Nadab and Abihu, should also be priests. In Leviticus 10:1–2, we see Nadab and Abihu offering up incense to God, but they chose not to offer it up in the way God had instructed them:

> Then Nadab and Abihu, the sons of Aaron, each took his censer and put fire in it, put incense on it, and offered profane fire before the Lord, which He had not commanded them. So fire went out from the Lord and devoured them, and they died before the Lord.

God killed them because they did not follow the specific liturgical instructions He had set down for them. Other passages from later in this same chapter indicate that Nadab and Abihu were probably drunk, and that may well have been what caused them not to get coals from the sacred fire in the Tabernacle to use for the incense. It is not their drunkenness that is indicated when God kills them, however, but rather that they offered "profane [or strange] fire."

In speaking of this incident, the great second-century Christian teacher St. Irenaeus of Lyons has this to say:

> And the heretics, indeed, who bring strange fire to the altar of God—namely, strange doctrines—shall be burned up by the fire from heaven, as were Nadab and Abiud. But such as rise up in opposition to the truth, and exhort others against the Church of God, [shall] remain among those in hell, being swallowed up by an earthquake, even as those who were with Chore, Dathan, and Abiron.[6]

Irenaeus identifies this kind of transgression with heresy itself, closely linking heretical doctrine with heretical worship.

The use of "heretics" and "strange doctrines" (i.e., the things taught by heretics) should not be understood here as a judgmental condemnation by Irenaeus against people who happen to have different opinions. He uses strong language for heretics precisely because he believes they are leading people away from the path of holiness and communion with God—eternal life with God is at stake. It may seem jarring in the twenty-first century to read talk of "fire from heaven"; however, Irenaeus is speaking not as a member of a dominant Christian establishment wagging its finger at those who refuse to submit, but as a teacher in a persecuted Church. He

sees the stakes as quite high, and he himself was eventually
martyred for his faith by the government of the time.

In the New Testament, we also see references to liturgical worship, both Jesus and His apostles participating in
Jewish liturgy but also in Christian liturgy, most especially
the Eucharist. While passages such as Christ's revelation to
His disciples at Emmaus in Luke 24 do not depict a fully
developed liturgical rite, we nevertheless see the clear New
Testament theme of the "breaking of the bread," which is
a eucharistic reference. And in Acts 2:42 we read that "they
continued steadfastly in the apostles' doctrine and fellow-
ship, in breaking of bread, and in [the] prayers."

Admittedly, the New Testament never gives the kind of
detailed information about worship for Christians that we
find for the Jews in Leviticus. However, we would be mis-
taken to conclude from this that Christians began immediately instituting a radically different kind of worship than
had been practiced in Judaism, especially since Acts 2 also
indicates that the disciples of Christ were "daily with one
accord in the temple." Going to the temple in Jerusalem
was something the first Christians were all doing together.
It therefore makes sense that Christian worship as it was
revealed in the history of the next few centuries would be
distinctly liturgical, sacrificial, and suffused with the language of Scripture, most especially of the Psalms—it strongly
resembled Jewish worship.

As the Church emerged from its Jewish context, there was

no radical break in the nature of worship. Instead, the two main services for Christians developed as modifications of a synagogue service, with emphasis on reading Scripture, teaching, and learning, along with a transformed temple service, with its emphasis on sacrifice. Eventually, these two merged together to become the Divine Liturgy (in Western Christianity, the Mass), the primary eucharistic worship service of the Church. All liturgical Christians throughout the world—which even in our own day still is the majority of Christians—and nearly every Christian in all of history, up until roughly the eighteenth century, worshiped with this basic pattern.

Those outside Christian circles may find it curious that some Christians worship according to this liturgical pattern while other Christians urge a radical break from it. Which makes more sense? From the Orthodox point of view, those who urge a radical break with centuries of liturgical Christianity must either be unaware of the liturgical character of worship in most of Christian history, or they must regard themselves as being more authoritative than the disciples of the apostles and all the generations of Christians, across numerous cultures and times, from then until just recently.

If those who believe that Christian worship should no longer be liturgical are right, they need to explain why liturgical worship was the norm for so many cultures over such a vast span of time, and why Christians should now completely abandon that tradition in favor of something dedicated instead to spontaneity and personal fulfillment. The forms of this new type of Christianity do not express the timeless eternity of the liturgy as it is depicted, for instance, in the biblical references to worship in heaven (such as in Is. 6 and Rev. 6), but are rather patterned after forms borrowed from academia, theater, and pop music.

In the Bible, we never see spontaneity or a private sense of fulfillment as a measure for correct worship. We see the opposite—that God has given specific instructions, and He expects them to be followed. This does not mean there have not been changes in some of the details of liturgical worship over the centuries, both within pre-Christian Judaism and within Christian worship, but there is nevertheless a direct continuity of worship from the earliest years of Christian life to the Orthodox Church of today.

This truth is important for anyone trying to figure out what the point of worship is and whether they want to do it. How can you figure those things out if there are so many different things all going by the name *worship*? From the Orthodox point of view, authentic Christian worship is what's found throughout most of Christian history.

WORSHIP IN CHRISTIAN HISTORY

The earliest written details we have for Christian worship after the New Testament come from the writings of St. Justin Martyr, an early convert to Christianity from pagan philosophy. His *First Apology*, which explains Christianity to the surrounding pagan society, was written about the year 150, possibly as late as 155 (*apology* here means "explanation," not "asking for forgiveness"). In it, he describes the standard Sunday worship service:

> And on the day which is called the Sun's Day there is an assembly
> of all who live in the towns or country; and the memoirs of the
> Apostles or the writings of the prophets are read, as much as
> time permits. When the reader has finished, the president gives
> a discourse, admonishing us and exhorting us to imitate these
> excellent examples. Then we all rise together and offer prayers; and,
> as I said above, on the conclusion of our prayer, bread is brought
> and wine and water; and the president similarly offers up prayers
> and thanksgivings [literally eucharists] to the best of his power,
> and the people assent with Amen[7].

From this brief passage from St. Justin, we see a clear liturgical pattern. First, this is a gathering of all the believers in the area. They are not off by themselves, but worshiping corporately. The service is also held on Sunday. A passage is read from apostolic writings or from the Old Testament, followed by a sermon. After that, joint prayers are offered, concluding with the offering of the bread and wine mixed with water, over which the president of the gathering offers up prayers and thanksgivings, with the assent of the people.

This witness from the middle of the second century has just described exactly what is seen on Sunday morning at every Orthodox church throughout the world. Was this pattern derived from reading Justin—that is, did the Orthodox try to recreate what Justin described? No, Justin is simply witnessing to the same continuous, unbroken tradition of liturgical worship that has been handed down from the apostles.

St. Ignatius of Antioch, the third bishop of that city, who was a disciple of the Apostle John and was martyred early in the second century, although not giving many details of the Sunday liturgy, has this to say about it: "Take great care to keep one Eucharist. For there is one Flesh of our Lord Jesus Christ and one cup to unite us by His Blood; one sanctuary, as there is one bishop, together with the presbytery and the deacons, my fellow-servants. Thus all your acts may be done according to God's will."[8] Ignatius here identifies the Eucharist not only with church unity but also with the ordained offices of the Church—the bishop, presbyters, and deacons. Ignatius received his instruction in Christian life from an apostle, and this is the kind of worship he practiced.

Likewise, the *Didache,* a second-century document giving practical advice on church life, says this: "And on the Lord's own day [i.e., Sunday] gather yourselves together and break bread and hold the Eucharist, first confessing your transgressions, that your sacrifice may be pure" (14). The Didache goes on to quote from Malachi 1, indicating that the sacrifice of the Eucharist for Christians is a fulfillment of Old Testament prophecy. Thus, far from being "Judaizers" (i.e., Christians attempting to imitate Judaism) in continuing with liturgical worship, early Christians instead understood that they were the New Israel, fulfilling what had been given by God to the Jews and transformatively bringing it to its proper completion. While there had formerly been animal sacrifices that had to be repeated, there was now one Sacrifice, which needs no repetition but is re-presented again and again in the Eucharist.

This re-presentation is itself presented in Scripture, particularly in the phrase "do this in remembrance of Me," found in both Luke 22:19 and 1 Corinthians 11:24. In both of these passages, the word for *remembrance* is not the Greek word meaning "recall," which is *mneia*. Rather, the word used there is *anamnesis*, which means "to make present by means of memory." Anamnesis is invocation—by doing this act, the Church is invoking the very presence of that which it remembers, making truly present at this moment something from the past. Thus, the Eucharist brings worshipers to the Cross and the Resurrection, or rather, it brings the Cross and the Resurrection to them.

In Orthodox worship, we do not merely think about these events as past, but we experience them as present. That is anamnesis, and that is why the Eucharist is not a symbolic eating and drinking, a sign of an absent presence, but is rather the re-presenting of that same reality. It is no wonder that early Christians believed in the true presence of Christ in the Eucharist, taught as they were by St. Paul, who said in 1 Corinthians 10:16–17: "The cup of blessing which we bless, is it not the communion of the blood of Christ? The bread which we break, is it not the communion of the body of Christ? For we, though many, are one bread and one body; for we all partake of that one bread."

St. Irenaeus says this about the reality of the Eucharist:

We offer to Him what is His own, suitably proclaiming the communion and unity of flesh and spirit. For as the bread, which comes from the earth, receives the invocation of God, and then it is no longer common bread but Eucharist, consists of two things, an earthly and a heavenly; so our bodies, after partaking of the Eucharist, are no longer corruptible, having the hope of the eternal resurrection.[9]

And St. Ignatius warns his readers in terms of the Eucharist how they can spot certain heretics called Docetists, who believed Jesus was not truly human but only appeared to be: "They abstain from Eucharist and prayer, because they do not confess that the Eucharist is the Flesh of our Savior Jesus Christ, who suffered for our sins, whom the Father raised up by His goodness."[10]

WORSHIP IN ECCLESIOLOGY

Another thing the Eucharist implies is that there must be a Church. There has to be a gathering, presided over by someone who speaks the prayers during which the bread and wine, through anamnesis, are changed by God into the Body and Blood of Christ. For the Orthodox Christian, this is why there is "organized religion." All of this cannot be accomplished simply by any person who wants it to be so.

St. Justin, whose description of the basic outline of the Sunday liturgy we read earlier, also writes that the Eucharist is not given to just anyone:

> And this food is called among us Eucharist, of which no one is allowed to partake but the man who believes that the things which we teach are true, and who has been washed with the washing that is for the remission of sins, and unto regeneration, and who is so living as Christ has enjoined. For not as common bread and common drink do we receive these; but in like manner as Jesus Christ our Saviour, having been made flesh by the Word of God, had both flesh and blood for our salvation, so likewise have we been taught that the food which is blessed by the prayer of His word, and from which our blood and flesh by transmutation are nourished, is the flesh and blood of that Jesus who was made flesh. For the apostles, in the memoirs composed by them, which are called Gospels, have thus delivered unto us what was enjoined upon them; that Jesus took bread, and when He had given thanks, said, 'This do ye in remembrance of Me, this is My body;' and that, after the same manner, having taken the cup and given thanks, He said, 'This is My blood;' and gave it to them alone.[11]

For Justin, to partake of the Eucharist, one not only has to be a member of the Church by baptism, but one also has to believe the teachings of the Church and be living the life of the Church as Christ taught. Why is this line drawn? Why does he not invite everyone to communion, but only those who are prepared through all these means? It is because this is not "common bread and common drink," and, as St. Paul warned in 1 Corinthians 11, eating and drinking the

Body and Blood of Christ in an unworthy manner can lead to sickness, death, and even damnation. Doesn't that make sense, if the Eucharist is truly the Body and Blood of Jesus Christ, connecting us directly to God Himself?

Likewise, if Christ gave the first Eucharist to the apostles alone, and not to just anyone who claimed to follow Him, it doesn't make sense for those who have departed from the communities founded by the Apostles, or who have never belonged to them, to receive the Eucharist. The line drawn is always at baptism, which constitutes entry into a real community, and that baptism can only be received from someone already in that community. And communion also requires ongoing presence within the community. Just as the Apostles traveled in order to ordain men as bishops (Titus 1), baptism also requires a real connection with the community, not just assent by proclaiming a common faith. Even Paul, who received revelation from God, went first to Ananias to be baptized and then to the Twelve Apostles for their approval, because he had to be received by the Church. He couldn't set up his own new denomination based on his private experiences.

This New Testament experience is the source of traditional Christian ecclesiology (the theology of the Church), which includes the scandal of the Eucharist—including its "closed" character, that not everyone can receive it. There was never a point in early Christian history when any person who walked up to the chalice could receive Holy

Communion just by making a profession of faith. He had to become a full member of the community. The *Didache* also bears witness to this: "But let no one eat or drink from your Eucharist except those who are baptized in the Lord's Name. For the Lord also has spoken concerning this: Do not give what is holy to dogs [Matt. 7:6]" (9.5). At this very early point in Christian history, the variety of baptisms and the numerous Christian sects we have in our own day did not yet exist, but it is clear that the writer regarded it necessary to be part of church life in order to partake of the Eucharist.

Additionally, as we saw earlier with Ignatius's insistence that there be only "one Eucharist," connected with the "one Flesh of our Lord Jesus Christ," "one sanctuary," and "one bishop," the image presented from all these early Christian writers is of one concrete community that a person is either part of or outside of. No one can legitimately set up his own community independently of those that exist within the apostolic succession. If not just anyone can receive the Eucharist, then not just anyone can lead its celebration, either. A minister of the sacrament has to have authoritative succession from the apostles. Only those ordained by the apostles and their successors from generation to generation have the authority to celebrate the Eucharist.

Earlier we quoted St. Irenaeus when he refers to the sons of Aaron with their "strange fire." The context of his remarks is what it means to break from the Church. In his view, breaking from the Church comes about mainly through breaking faith with the successors to the apostles, most especially on doctrinal grounds. He writes:

> *Wherefore it is incumbent to obey the priests who are in the Church,—those who, as I have shown, possess the succession from the apostles; those who, together with the succession of the episcopate, have received the certain gift of truth, according to the good pleasure of the Father. But [it is also incumbent] to hold in suspicion others who depart from the primitive succession, and assemble themselves together in any place whatsoever, [looking upon them] either as heretics of perverse minds, or as schismatics puffed up and self-pleasing, or again as hypocrites, acting thus for the sake of lucre and vainglory. For all these have fallen from the truth. And the heretics, indeed, who bring strange fire to the altar of God—namely, strange doctrines—shall be burned up by the fire from heaven, as were Nadab and Abiud. But such as rise up in opposition to the truth, and exhort others against the Church of God, [shall] remain among those in hell, being swallowed up by an earthquake, even as those who were with Chore, Dathan, and Abiron. But those who cleave asunder, and separate the unity of the Church, [shall] receive from God the same punishment as Jeroboam did.[12]*

These strong words from Irenaeus show not only the seriousness of heresy but also that it is not acceptable to "depart from the primitive succession, and assemble . . . together in any place whatsoever." This "assembling" is gathering for worship.

Because the Eucharist, the center of Christian worship from the earliest times, is a concrete, local celebration, that means the Church is a concrete, local reality. The idea of an "invisible" Church, one where people can be true followers of Christ without having any connection to the Eucharist as celebrated within the apostolic community, is foreign to the earliest Christians. St. Irenaeus goes so far as to stake his own doctrinal orthodoxy not on any text he's mastered, but on the Eucharist itself, saying, "our opinion is in accordance with the Eucharist, and the Eucharist in turn establishes our opinion."[13]

WHY GO TO CHURCH?

The previous two sections have tried to establish what authentic Christian worship looks like. Worship is so key to Orthodox Christian spiritual life because we believe that in worship we meet God.

From our brief survey of biblical and early Christian witnesses, we can say a number of things about what Christian worship was like in the earliest years of church life, and we can also see from the Orthodox Church of today that these same unchanging characteristics remain. We worship God not because He has any need for praise, not because He needs to feel good about Himself, not because He needs us in any way, but because we inherently need communion with Him—this is the great thirst. Our nature requires this communion for our wholeness, for spiritual health, because God created us not to be isolated individuals, but rather communing persons, communing with each other and most especially with Him.

Worship in the Christian context, therefore, is not merely

someone telling God how great He is or putting himself in servitude. It is rather the total self-giving of the human person to the divine Persons, receiving the divine Trinitarian life in return, the connection and union of the created with the Uncreated, yet without fusion of the one into the other.

In order to make this union possible, we who are created need access to something created that is united to the Uncreated. It is only in the Incarnation of Christ that this is possible, because He is both uncreated and created, having taken created human nature into His uncreated divine Person. It is in His humanity that we have access to divinity. We can't touch divinity without that humanity. That connection we make through createdness to uncreatedness was in ancient times symbolized through the blood of animals, but since the coming of the Son of God is now made present and real in the Body and Blood of Christ. This becomes truly present for the worshiper by means of anamnesis, the remembrance that goes beyond mere recall and becomes invocation.

We also saw that liturgical worship was the norm for the Jews and also for the early Christians. A faith that involves human persons, who are composed of both body and soul, must embrace both body and soul. There has always been a physical aspect of being spiritual, an intuition understood not just by Jews and Christians, but by pagans and nearly every religion in the history of mankind. God also cares about the actual shape of our worship, not because He has a favorite "style," but because we worship Him on His terms, in accordance with the way He created human persons to commune with the divine Persons. For the Orthodox, the shape that worship takes is not a matter of taste, but a matter of what actually works according to God's design.

For the Orthodox, worship is not merely something Christians do, but what they are—indeed, it is what all human beings are. It is only in the act of worship that the human person is truly himself. It is only in the act of worship that the Church is truly constituted. The episcopacy, the priesthood, and the diaconate are only truly what they are in the context of worship. These roles are not those of administrators but rather those of celebrants at the divine services. Ultimately, everything Orthodox Christians do has reference to and is defined by the Eucharist and by the divine services surrounding it. For us, there is no Christianity without the Eucharist.

It therefore makes sense that the center and height of Christian life should be the Eucharist, which has profound ecclesiological and doctrinal implications. There is no Eucharist outside the unity of the one Church, and there is also no Eucharist outside doctrinal orthodoxy, which is why St. Irenaeus said, "our opinion is in accordance with the Eucharist, and the Eucharist in turn establishes our opinion."

The reason to go to church is worship. While it is possible to think about God, to love God, to learn about God, and even to praise God outside of a church—and there can be a worshipful aspect to those actions—the fullness of worship is only to be found in the eucharistic community, whose worship includes not only those moments when the Eucharist is received but also the whole liturgical tradition.

Even when Holy Communion is not received at a church service, all Orthodox worship presupposes a worship life centered on the Eucharist. The inherent physicality of all Orthodox services, their involvement of the body, puts us into contact with the God who became incarnate, taking on a body. Orthodox worship includes much more than the Eucharist received at the Divine Liturgy, and the liturgical cycle includes many non-eucharistic services, such as Vespers, Matins, and the Hours.

Orthodox Christian spiritual life encompasses everything in life, not just church services, though the services are at the center of life. Orthodox Christians certainly do see God out in the depth of the woods, in the glory and power of a sunset, at the soaring peaks of mountains, and in the unfathomable vastness of the oceans. But what all of that brings us back to over and over again is the ultimate fulfillment of God connecting to us in creation, which is the Eucharist. And even the Eucharist itself, which begins as wheat and grapes grown in fields, encompasses the creation. It is not apart from it.

Authentic worship requires community, and because the community is led in its worship by an ordained sacramental priesthood, the *fullness* of worship just isn't available outside the community. It would be like a child out on his own insisting that he is a family. He can't become a family when he grows up, either, as long as he's by himself. Just as family life requires a family, Orthodox worship always involves a community. And just as a family needs parents, the church needs its priesthood. All of these elements work together to bring us into communion with Christ, and through Him and in Him, with His Father and the Holy Spirit.

So why should anyone want to go to church? Orthodox Christians go to church to connect directly with God—not because He is unavailable elsewhere in creation, but because He makes Himself most intensely available in the worship He set in place, and in a unique way in the Eucharist.

And if we are going to go looking for the Eucharist and the whole Orthodox spirituality that surrounds it, we have to have some sense of the best way to find them. And so we ask: Whom can we trust?

CHAPTER FOUR

The Mystery of the Church

Whom Can We Trust?

And what the dead had no speech for, when living,
They can tell you, being dead: the communication
Of the dead is tongued with fire beyond the language of
   the living.

                    T. S. Eliot, "Little Gidding"

WHERE DID THE BIBLE COME FROM?

In the year AD 367, the Christian bishop of the Egyptian city of Alexandria had a problem.

He was a veteran of the doctrinal debates that had raged throughout the fourth century, and so it only made sense that he had a concern for the welfare of his flock, most especially that they not be led astray by teachings that deviated from the original Christian faith. His particular concern in that year was that some people were circulating writings

AN INTRODUCTION TO GOD

that claimed to be from the apostles, mixing them in with the books he regarded as authentically apostolic.

When he sat down to write his Paschal letter for that year, his greetings on the feast of Christ's resurrection (Easter), he decided to write out a list of books he considered to be proper for the Christians in his churches to read, most especially to be read aloud during church services. Here's what he wrote:

> Again it is not tedious to speak of the [books] of the New Testament. These are, the four Gospels, according to Matthew, Mark, Luke, and John. Afterwards, the Acts of the Apostles and Epistles (called Catholic), seven, viz. of James, one; of Peter, two; of John, three; after these, one of Jude. In addition, there are fourteen Epistles of Paul, written in this order. The first, to the Romans; then two to the Corinthians; after these, to the Galatians; next, to the Ephesians; then to the Philippians; then to the Colossians; after these, two to the Thessalonians, and that to the Hebrews; and again, two to Timothy; one to Titus; and lastly, that to Philemon. And besides, the Revelation of John[14].

Those who know the New Testament well will have counted exactly the twenty-seven books of the New Testament found in all Bibles today. The Alexandrian bishop says of these books that they are "fountains of salvation, that they who thirst may be satisfied with the living words they contain. In these alone is proclaimed the doctrine of godliness. Let no man add to these, neither let him take ought from these."

The bishop's name was Athanasius, and he is known to

Christian history as St. Athanasius the Great. Forty-two years before, while he was still a deacon, he was the hero of the great Council of Nicea, the First Ecumenical Council, which delineated in clear terms the core of Christian doctrine, most especially that Jesus Christ is the God of the universe. What's particularly remarkable about Athanasius's list of the books of the New Testament is that it is the first time known to history when those twenty-seven books are listed together as a Christian biblical canon.

Many Christians claim they simply follow what the Bible says, that the proper understanding of the Bible and all Christian doctrine is available to anyone who is honest and serious, and it helps to have access to the original biblical languages of Hebrew and Greek. But how would such a view have fared in the time of Athanasius? The question "What is the Bible?" had not been answered, and there is little evidence Christians even asked that question until more than one hundred years after Jesus' resurrection.

Yet if Christians say that we believe the Bible, that its writings are, as Athanasius wrote, "fountains of salvation," then it is critical that we understand where the Bible came from and what the context of that process was. Where did the content of the Bible come from? How did Christians function for more than three hundred years without a set canon for the New Testament? What did the people who defined the canon believe? Where did they get the authority to make such an awesome determination?

WHO'S IN CHARGE HERE?

When modern man encounters the Orthodox Church, he may be struck first of all by its structure. Often, instead of questions concerning the core of what the Church teaches and how the spiritual life works, inquiries are first made concerning the ranks and duties of clergy, who is allowed to be ordained, where the bishop, archbishop, and patriarch happen to reside, and so on. These are essentially political questions: How is the Church organized and administered? Who answers to whom? Who has the power? Who's in charge here?

The seeker looking into Christianity wants to know the answers to these questions because he wants to know who can be trusted to teach him what Christianity really is. And someone who's already a Christian is interested in these issues, too, because there are many people claiming to speak for Christianity. Which one is right? Who's in charge?

These questions are not surprising, considering how much energy modern society puts into the political process. The first solution to so many problems is presumed to be through political power and policy. But the Orthodox Church doesn't look at things that way. Within Orthodoxy, there is certainly power, but that power does not belong to any church member, except to one, and that is Jesus Christ Himself. Within the Church, the only power active is the power of the Holy Trinity—the Father, Son, and Holy Spirit.

Power is different from authority, though many people

confuse the two. To have the power to do something is to have the inherent capability to perform the task. To have the authority to do something is to be authorized by someone to carry out a task. What the Church has is authority, given to her by Christ Himself through His apostles. But not even the apostles had power. They only had authority. When we see power coming out of them, as when they raised the dead or healed the sick, we are seeing the power of God, who has given them the authority to be conduits of that power. Likewise, when a person is baptized, when forgiveness is given at confession, or when bread and wine are changed to the Body and Blood of Christ, it is not the priest or bishop who has the power to do those things. His own power is useless, but he becomes a conduit for the power of God.

So the question we are addressing in this chapter is really about authority, not about power. God has all the power in the Church. But He grants authority in how His power is applied, and if the authority is abused, then the power may operate independently or, more often, through another person granted that authority. For instance, a wicked priest cannot withhold God's forgiveness from someone who is truly repentant.

So how has God granted this authority within the Church? And how is it supposed to be used? What is it for? How does God's wisdom and healing—His power—actually get to us in the Church? In order to understand this question, let's first examine two non-Orthodox approaches found in the Christian world, first because they may be more familiar to you, and also so that we may clear out of the way as many misconceptions about the Orthodox teaching as possible.

THE RULE OF MEN: AUTHORITY AS EXTERNAL OFFICE

The question we asked earlier—"Who's in charge here?"—is perhaps most easily answered by a Roman Catholic Christian. Who's in charge for him? It's a complex question, but in the most general sense, the one in charge for the Roman Catholic is the Pope of Rome, who is regarded as personally infallible when he speaks from his throne on issues of doctrine and morals. He also is believed to have universal, immediate jurisdiction over every Christian on Earth. His authority extends to everything and everyone within the Roman Catholic Church and (if only they would acknowledge it) to every Christian. His infallibility is solemnly and dogmatically defined as not relying on the consent of the Church.

His authority adheres to him by virtue of his being the Pope of Rome. Authority within the Roman Catholic Church then flows from him in a pyramid shape, through Roman Catholic bishops, then to the priests, and so on. There are a number of stops along the way, such as the Vatican Curia, the College of Cardinals, regional councils of bishops, and so on, but it's all a pretty straightforward structure. If there is a question about what it truly means to be a Roman Catholic, one could theoretically just ask the Pope, and that would be that. Or, as a popular saying in Roman Catholicism goes, "Rome has spoken; the matter is settled" (which is actually a misquote from St. Augustine's *Sermon 131*).

This kind of thing appeals to the mind accustomed to working in rational contexts. Where is the authority? Where can I go for the answer? There must be some place to look this up! I need to know right now! It's much easier to get answers straight from the horse's mouth when the horse is dressed all in white and living in an identifiable location in central Italy. He also has his own webpage, which includes the *Catechism of the Catholic Church*, a compendium of the official teaching of the Roman Catholic Magisterium. It's all quite neat and tidy, organized religion at its finest.

By contrast, Orthodox Christians are sometimes known for not being an "organized" religion. While that might be an amusing way of putting it, I think there's something to it that goes beyond cultural foibles and jokes about "Greek time" or "Middle Eastern time" (people especially from Mediterranean cultural backgrounds often seem to show up to things chronically late, including church services). Is there some *theological* reason why the temporal, earthly aspect of Orthodox authority structures can sometimes seem so disorganized, especially compared with the Roman Catholic hierarchy?

We'll examine that question more closely in a moment,

but let's turn our attention back to the common Western cultural understanding of authority as being embodied in an external office held by a particular person. If we consider this question historically, we can see the rise of the feudal political system in medieval Europe, which is predicated upon a complex web of personal loyalties to feudal lordships. That system eventually came to define the structure of the Roman Catholic Church, and bishops became landholders and feudal lords in their own right. The Pope eventually came to have his own lands over which he was the secular ruler, and even led armies into battle for the purpose of defending and expanding his territory. Even today, when the Roman Catholic hierarchy has mostly been stripped of its secular power, the Pope is still a secular leader over the microstate of Vatican City, located inside Rome, with its own police force, currency, and government offices. This is externalized authority, the rule of men over other men, including the ability to use violence to reinforce that authority.

As the Pope eventually lost secular control over what were called the Papal States, the Roman Catholic emphasis on externalized secular power was replaced by one on externalized religious power, especially in the form of a strong threat of eternal damnation if the Pope was not obeyed. Though this language has been softened over the past century, we may nevertheless recall the various statements Rome has made over the centuries about how it is necessary to salvation for every human person that he be subject to the

Pope of Rome (e.g., in the document *Unam Sanctam* in 1302).

Orthodox Christianity doesn't take that approach to authority. Authority is certainly vested in persons holding offices—the bishop has the authority to ordain clergy, for instance. But this is not an externalized authority, and it does not have the force of violence to back it up (despite a few instances in church history when some wicked bishops have tried). Nor has loyalty and obedience to any particular man, even a patriarch, been doctrinally and solemnly declared as a criterion for salvation.

And though Orthodoxy has always understood those who hold authoritative positions within the Church as being in some sense mediators for the people, they are not gateways to God. There is not, as in Roman Catholicism, a treasury of merits stored up by Christ and the saints that the hierarchy may dispense as they see fit for our salvation. In Orthodoxy, no single clerical official—whether he is a pope, patriarch, archbishop, metropolitan, bishop, priest, or deacon—is absolutely essential to salvation.

THE RULE OF LAW:
AUTHORITY AS EXTERNAL TEXTS

When the Protestant Reformation exploded onto the scene in Western Europe in the sixteenth century, not only did the religious landscape radically fragment and change, but the political reality transformed, as well. It was the beginning of the formation of democracy and the nation state as we now understand them. At the Reformation's core was the belief that authority should not reside in mighty men and women, whether "lords temporal" (feudal nobles) or "lords spiritual" (the clergy), but that true authority, and even political power, belonged to the populace, specifically to each person. There is something in this intuition that resonates with Orthodoxy, but the religious doctrine behind the democratic political tradition that came out of the Protestant Reformation is not compatible with the teachings of the Orthodox Church.

The apparent problem was that authority residing in the offices of men was too susceptible to corruption, especially when those men were understood as the gatekeepers of the Kingdom of Heaven. Some of the Reformers believed authority had to be decentralized and codified in a manner that would make it impervious to corruption. For the Protestant Reformation, the mechanism that accomplished this was the doctrine of *sola scriptura*.

Sola scriptura means "by Scripture alone," and its purpose was to locate all authority in the text of the Bible. Instead of an externalized *hierarchical* authority, this new Reformation dogma created an externalized *textual* authority. Christians were expected to be obedient not to authoritative people, but to an authoritative text. This sensibility leads naturally to the modern idea of rule by law rather than persons. No one is above the law, and there should be no exceptions to the law.

On its surface, this sounds pretty good. Christians agreed that the Bible was reliable, came from the apostles, and represented true Christian belief. But the problem comes when actually applying what the Bible says, because all texts need interpretation. That lands us back at the question of who has the authority to make a correct interpretation. It gets even worse when we consider that *sola scriptura* is not actually taught by the Bible. Thus *sola scriptura* violates its own principle. It also ignores the centuries at the beginning of Christian history when the canon of the Bible hadn't even been settled. You can't just go by the Bible when you don't even know what the Bible is.

The problem with this model of authority is that it keeps authority as an external force. In this case, the external force is a text rather than persons. But of course, it still ends up in the hands of people, since Christians will inevitably have leadership when they organize with each other, and also because even a Christian privately reading the Bible by himself will apply interpretation to it.

THE ORTHODOX APPROACH: HOLY TRADITION

The Orthodox Christian approach to authority is not external, but rather *internal*. The inner life of the church community is the basis for everything the Christian does, whether it is his interpretation of Holy Scripture, his repentance for sins, or his obedience to the Church. What does this mean? How does an internal authority function differently from an external one?

Fundamentally, it means that everything is done out of freedom. There are no demands put on the believer that he does not put on himself. He is not threatened with anything if he fails to comply with either an external clerical office or an external text. But the internality of the Church's authority is not *primarily* within the individual believer but rather within the body of the Church as a whole, expressed in what is called *Holy Tradition*.

One may object that a group of people is not a reliable place to seat authority, especially a large group of people spread across twenty centuries of church life. Those who would raise this objection, when considering the idea of church tradition, may understand tradition as something that grows and alters over time. But this objection is usually based on certain unspoken assumptions.

One of those assumptions is that tradition must necessarily be unreliable, because it is a purely human construct. But if we examine the notion of tradition as discussed within the New Testament itself, we will find that this assumption is incorrect.

There are thirteen places where the New Testament uses the word *tradition*—in Greek, *paradosis*. In ten of those places, it is clear that tradition is a negative thing, coming from fallible humanity. But in the other three (1 Cor. 11:2; 2 Thess.

2:15; 3:6), tradition is lauded by the apostles as coming from God. In the second one, 2 Thessalonians 2:15, Paul not only lauds the tradition of God but commands the Thessalonians to follow it: "Therefore, brethren, stand fast and hold the traditions which you were taught, whether by word or our epistle." In verse 3:6, he tells believers to withdraw themselves from those who refuse to follow the apostolic tradition: "But we command you, brethren, in the name of our Lord Jesus Christ, that you withdraw from every brother who walks disorderly and not according to the tradition which he received from us." The Bible makes a distinction between the traditions of men and the tradition of God, which is what the apostles preach and teach.

Tradition in its most basic sense is something that is "handed over." This is the meaning of both the Greek *paradosis* and the Latin *traditionem*, from which our English word *tradition* comes. The Orthodox Christian understanding of Holy Tradition is that it is the life in faith handed over by Christ to the apostles, then handed over by them to their disciples, from one generation to the next, without any addition, subtraction, or alteration. Holy Tradition is therefore not something that can grow or change over time.

The second unspoken assumption made by those who object to the idea of Christian tradition is that the Church is not being guided reliably by Christ. But from the Orthodox point of view, Christ not only guides the Church, builds it, and preserves it from defeat, as He promised in Matthew

16:18, but He is actually the Head of the Church and its chief member. There is therefore no need for an earthly head or vicar of Christ for the Church, as with the Roman Catholic papacy. Christ is not absent from His Church, and from within it He preserves the Church as a whole from error. This is why in the Nicene Creed, which was adopted in the fourth century as an expression of core Christian doctrine, the Church itself is an article of faith: "I believe in one, holy, catholic and apostolic Church." How can the Christian "believe in" the Church? It is because Christ is in charge within His Church, and He is completely reliable.

In a practical sense, if Christ were not guiding the Church, then there would be no way to know whether the doctrine we hold to is in fact true. One may say that He guides all Christian believers, and that constitutes His guidance for the Church. But that is not how early Christians understood the Church, and they are authoritative because of their closeness to the source. Also, since so many modern Christians—even very smart, well-read, and sincere ones—disagree with each other over doctrine, how are we to identify whom Christ is guiding and who is being guided by his own opinion? If there is no reliable Church, then doctrine is a free-for-all, subject to the whims of persuasive writers and charismatic preachers. But if there is a reliable Church, one guided by Christ and preserved from error, then the question is how one locates it.

The Church is described in Scripture as the location

where we can know the truth, such as in 1 Timothy 3:15, where the Church is called "the pillar and ground of the truth." If the Church is not recognizable as a specific community with clear doctrine, then Paul's description of it as "the pillar and ground of the truth" is meaningless, because it is impractical. If the term *the Church* refers to all Christian believers everywhere, regardless of the contradictory doctrinal variation between them, then there is effectively no "pillar and ground of the truth." Everyone is simply left guessing, or perhaps dueling between themselves with smarter and smarter theology professors.

Some Christians assume everyone will agree on what Scripture means and what Christian life should be if only they are honest enough, smart enough, and educated enough. This is customarily contrasted with the papal model of Roman Catholicism, in which all arguments are settled by appealing to an institutional office. But unfortunately, neither model produces consistent, reliable results. The doctrinal chaos of modern Protestantism should be enough to dissuade anyone from believing that we need only be honest, smart, and well-read—unless we should believe that all the honest, smart, and well-read people are confined to one denomination. Likewise, the fact that there have been popes who were condemned as heretics (even by subsequent popes) should also warn one off placing that level of authority in the hands of one man, even a man bolstered by a very conservative and apparently immovable institutional structure.

One might argue that the *sola scriptura* approach of Protestantism is reliable because God is guiding the individual believer to make the right decisions. If he makes the wrong ones, he is obviously not serious enough about his faith. But that approach makes the prior assumption that the one making such judgments is himself divinely illumined. And so we're back where we started, with the honest but confused believer not knowing whom to trust, with everyone claiming to be led by the Holy Spirit yet not agreeing with one another on where the Spirit is leading.

Likewise, one might argue that the institution of the papacy is kept from error by the Holy Spirit. But if that is true, then why did Pope Honorius embrace the heresy of Monothelitism in the seventh century? And if he was right in embracing that doctrine, why did later popes condemn him for it? Who was being led by the Spirit—they or he? So we are back in the same quandary we are in with *sola scriptura* Protestantism, except that the pool of potential erroneous interpreters is much smaller.

In any event, my purpose here is not to delve deeply into the scriptural hermeneutics of either the Roman Catholic Church or Protestantism, but rather to introduce the Orthodox Christian concept of Holy Tradition. Orthodoxy does, indeed, make similar claims to being led by the Holy Spirit, but it places that leading in the Orthodox Church as a whole, not in the hands of a single bishop nor in those of the individual believer. This location for the Spirit's guidance is made not only because individual people prove again and again throughout history to be quite fallible, but because it is consistent with the history and experience of the Church as well as the testimony of Scripture. The Holy Spirit does lead the individual Christian, but because of his own fallibility, he needs the witness of the tradition of the Church to guide him.

THE BIBLE'S STORY

We said earlier that it was critical to know the history of the Bible within the Christian context if we are to understand the Orthodox Christian approach to biblical interpretation and to what Holy Tradition actually is. Let's first examine the Bible's history.

Right before Christ ascended into heaven, forty days after His resurrection from the dead, He said to the apostles:

> *"All authority has been given to Me in heaven and on earth. Go therefore and make disciples of all the nations, baptizing them in the name of the Father and of the Son and of the Holy Spirit, teaching them to observe all things that I have commanded you; and lo, I am with you always, even to the end of the age" (Matt. 28:18-20).*

These words, commonly called the "Great Commission," are notable in the context of what we're discussing for what they *don't* mention. In the Great Commission, Jesus doesn't mention the Bible. In fact, there is nowhere in the Gospels nor in the brief section at the beginning of the Book of Acts where He appears in which He makes any reference to the writing of the books of the New Testament. There is also no place anywhere in the New Testament (except the Book of Revelation, which was a late and reluctant inclusion in the biblical canon) where any of the writers says that Jesus told him to write his part of the Bible.

Therefore, what the Bible itself says about church authority does not mention the Bible. Rather, this is the picture we have: Christ calls the Twelve Apostles, one of whom (Judas) is lost along the way and later replaced by Matthias. For three years, Jesus teaches these men, and they journey with Him. They witness His suffering, death, resurrection, and ascension. At Pentecost they then receive the Holy Spirit, who, as Jesus predicted, leads them into all truth (John 16:13).

So the apostles have been led into all truth. With that truth, they begin preaching, first in Jerusalem, then in the surrounding area, and from there spreading out into much of the Roman Empire and even beyond. Along the way, they ordain bishops, presbyters, and deacons to lead the nascent Church.

There is a lot of scholarly conjecture regarding when the New Testament actually began to be written, but the earliest date I've seen for any of the books of the New Testament is AD 50 (for the Epistle of James and the two Pauline epistles to the Thessalonians). Therefore, the Church functioned for at least seventeen years from the time Jesus ascended into heaven until the time the New Testament began to be written. The latest books are probably those by the Apostle John, written during the decade following AD 90. Roughly sixty years elapsed between the Church's beginnings and the completion of the New Testament works.

What happened next, though, was not that St. John, the last living apostle (the rest had been martyred), combined his five works with the other twenty-two books of the New Testament, sent them off to a publisher, and then Christians everywhere immediately acquired copies and began asking what the Bible said when issues came up about how to live the Christian life. For one thing, books and publishers as we know them today did not exist; a single scroll containing the whole New Testament would have been impossibly unwieldy, and a copy would have taken months or years to create. But even if such a thing had been created, most people wouldn't have been able to read it anyway. Literacy was not very high at the time, and it was probably particularly low among Christians, since the Church attracted so many people from the lower classes.

What actually did happen next was nothing noteworthy, at least as far as the Bible was concerned. There was no attempt to gather together the writings of the apostles into a single collection, and hardly anyone was referring to them as Scripture. In fact, probably the first New Testament canon we know of was compiled by a man named Marcion, who in AD 145 created his own list. This list prominently featured a version of the Gospel of Luke that Marcion called *The Gospel of Christ*; ten of the traditional epistles of St. Paul; and (possibly) two epistles supposedly from Paul to the Laodiceans and the Alexandrians. Marcion had little use for any of the other writings we now recognize as the New Testament, and he rejected the Old Testament entirely, claiming that the God of the Jews was a vengeful, wrathful god who was not the same as the Father of Jesus Christ.

Even then, as we said at the beginning of this chapter, it was not until AD 367 that the Christian world first saw the list of the twenty-seven books of the New Testament as we now know them, contained in a pastoral letter by Athanasius, Bishop of Alexandria, to his churches. Thirty years later, a council in Carthage confirmed Athanasius's canon, and the canon of the New Testament was generally settled around the fourth and fifth centuries. The Church therefore functioned for about three hundred years without anyone being able to get a straight answer to the question, "What does the Bible say?" There was no Bible, not as we now understand it.

What guided the Church's life during those years? And, perhaps most intriguingly, how were the twenty-seven books that now constitute the New Testament sifted out from among the many dozens of writings claiming to come from the apostles? On what authority did someone like Athanasius make such a determination, since he couldn't just check his Bible for the answers?

SCRIPTURE IN TRADITION
AND AS TRADITION

In the late second century, Irenaeus (whom we mentioned in the previous chapter) undertook, as Athanasius would two hundred years later, to protect his flock from dangerous teachings. When defending against the heresies of the Gnostics, Irenaeus could not simply open up his Bible and refute them with scriptural quotations. Though he was familiar with many of the writings that would become the New Testament, there was no Bible. Although those writings existed, not all of them were widely available, and it was not clear at that time that those writings were destined to be considered Scripture. Irenaeus had to use a different strategy, the strategy which prevails in the Orthodox Church to this day.

When addressing the Gnostics, Irenaeus did not merely quote Scripture, because his opponents were also quoting Scripture. Rather, he appealed to the *regula fidei*, the "rule of faith." This phrase did not simply mean that he had faith that he was right and they were wrong. Rather, his phrase referred to the faith of the Church, the Holy Tradition that had been handed down by the apostles to their own disciples, on through the generations (though not very many generations at that point). For Irenaeus, the lifetime of Christ and the apostles was less removed from him in time than the American Civil War is from us. His main writing against heresy dates to less than 150 years after the Ascension, about

AD 180. And his teacher, Polycarp, was taught by the Apostle John.

The rule of faith was not a written creed. It was not compiled into writing anywhere. It was the ongoing life in Christ that Christians had been living in the Church for those 150 years. All indications from that period and for many centuries afterward are that, except for a handful of heretical groups, there was a striking unanimity among Christians about what to believe and how to live it, all without recourse to the biblical canon. Irenaeus knew heresy when he saw it, not because he could look up his doctrine in the Bible, but because he was steeped in the life of the Church. He immediately knew the visions of God the Gnostics taught were not what Christians had always believed. In his words:

> It is within the power of all, therefore, in every Church, who may wish to see the truth, to contemplate clearly the tradition of the apostles manifested throughout the whole world; and we are in a position to reckon up those who were by the apostles instituted bishops in the Churches, and [to demonstrate] the succession of these men to our own times; those who neither taught nor knew of anything like what these [heretics] rave about.[15]

He goes on to say, "And this is most abundant proof that there is one and the same vivifying faith, which has been preserved in the Church from the apostles until now, and handed down in truth."[16]

For Irenaeus, there was an ongoing succession from the apostles within the Christian churches that held to the rule of faith, and he was able to use that rule of faith as a measure to distinguish heresy from orthodoxy. This approach to Christian life is reminiscent of the admonition we read earlier from St. Paul: "Therefore, brethren, stand fast and hold the traditions which you were taught, whether by word or our epistle" (2 Thess. 2:15). The apostles were teaching the traditions of God, the Holy Tradition, both by word of mouth and by epistle.

This rule of faith is also the origin of the New Testament Scriptures and their canonical definition. What the apostles preached was the rule of faith, a deposit of Christian tradition given to those first Christians. Most of the time, they taught orally. Some of the time, they wrote down their teachings as letters to certain churches or persons. The context for all of this was the apostolic preaching, which constituted the Church and by which the Church continues to live and thrive. And the formation of the New Testament canon—which was a gradual process, not done by committee but by centuries of sifting, mainly in the context of worship services—was carried out according to the rule of faith given by the apostles.

The canon was not produced merely by asking which books had been written by apostles. After all, many books claimed to be from them. Even if it were absolutely known which books were apostolic, that would not give them automatic inclusion in the canon. There is, for instance, in 1 Corinthians 5:9, a reference to an earlier epistle of Paul to the

Corinthians. Likewise, in Colossians 4:16, Paul mentions his epistle to the Laodiceans, and Ephesians 3:3-4 may reference an earlier epistle to the Ephesians. These epistles have been lost to us, but even if we had them all today, they would not be included in the canon, because the Holy Tradition of the Church did not preserve and include them.

Holy Tradition is therefore the origin of the text of the Scriptures. Holy Tradition is also the origin of the canon of the Scriptures. The only proper way to understand the Scriptures is within the Holy Tradition that produced it.

Scriptural texts can be taken out of their proper context in the rule of faith to mean just about anything someone wants them to mean. Context was of great importance for another Christian pastor roughly contemporary with Athanasius in the fourth century: Basil the Great, the bishop of the city of Caesarea in Cappadocia (in modern Turkey). Basil explicitly takes on the question of what is normative for life in the Church and its relation with Scripture. He writes:

> Of the doctrines and injunctions kept by the Church, some we have from instruction. But some we have received, from Apostolic Tradition, by succession in private [i.e., unwritten tradition]. Both the former and the latter have one and the same force for piety, and this will be contradicted by no one who has ever so little knowledge in the ordinances of the Church; for were we to dare to reject unwritten customs, as if they had no great importance, we should insensibly mutilate the Gospel, even in the most essential points, or, rather, for the teaching of the Apostles leave but an empty name.[17]

Thus, for Basil, if you ignore the unwritten traditions from the apostles, then you will not be able to understand properly the written ones, either. Instead, you "mutilate the Gospel."

In the centuries since Basil's time, many of the unwritten traditions that existed in his own era have been set down in written form (and he actually wrote a few of them down himself). That does not in any sense change their significance, however. In any event, there is not an official compendium of Holy Tradition published that could serve as an infallible written guide, because we are speaking of life, not texts. Orthodox Christianity is a dynamic union with God, not a systematic textbook.

Even though many have attempted to describe what it means to be united with God in Christ, there is nothing that could be written that can pass on that experience apart from an incarnate, direct handing over of what was received. We have many witnesses to Holy Tradition that stand alongside Scripture—the vast treasury of liturgical worship, the holy icons, the writings of the Church Fathers, the decrees of the Ecumenical Councils, and so on. But these should not be understood as being "parts" of Holy Tradition, as though it could simply be assembled from its parts. Likewise, while Scripture is central to Holy Tradition and in a real sense its most important element, Scripture does not function apart from Tradition, nor Tradition apart from Scripture.

WHOM CAN WE TRUST?

There is no specific "method" of Scripture interpretation that Orthodox Christianity has adopted exclusively. Why? It is because Orthodox Christianity is not a faith derived from the Bible, with scholars and theologians searching through its text like archaeologists trying to piece together some dead civilization from clues unearthed in the dust. Instead, the Bible is derived from the Orthodox faith. Historically, the Orthodox Church is the community established through the preaching of the apostles and then continuing from one generation to the next. In that process of tradition, handing down the same faith within the community, the New Testament was written. In that process of tradition, the New Testament was canonized. And in that same process, the New Testament is interpreted.

There is also nothing in the New Testament Scriptures that contradicts the tradition that produced and canonized them. Even if we were to look at the development of the biblical canon in purely cynical, secular terms, the Church would not have chosen books as Scripture that contradicted the Church's life. Why would early Christians have canonized texts that contradicted their own faith? For example, worship in the first centuries of Christianity was sacramental and liturgical. Administrative and liturgical authority was exercised through bishops, who ordained presbyters and deacons. Those who look at the Bible and see something else are not looking at it in the same way that those who canonized it did. Those who accept the canon of the New Testament, but not the faith of the canonizers, therefore find themselves in the position of accepting the canonizers' authority only when it comes to choosing the New Testament writings correctly, but not in anything else.

None of this means that God does not speak to individual believers. He certainly does. But the fallibility of every human being means that individual believers cannot of themselves be trusted as a normative guide to Christian life. Even looking into one's own heart unguided can be disastrous, for, as the Prophet Jeremiah said, "The heart is deceitful above all things, and desperately wicked; who can know it?" (Jer. 17:9). A trustworthy approach to the Scriptures and to all of Christian life will require something other than placing authority in an individual believer, whether layman or pope. We have to be part of something bigger than ourselves.

There is also no academic or other method for biblical interpretation that the Orthodox Church can exclusively sanction, because all such methods—the historical-critical method, textual criticism, fundamentalism, liberalism, etc.—reduce and alter the meaning of the Scriptures in ways that violate the rule of faith. There is simply the life of the Church, which has lasted for twenty centuries, teaching, living, and worshiping the same way with the same faith. Within that life, the Scriptures play a major role. We spoke of a few witnesses from the early centuries of Christianity, but a thorough examination of all the teachers throughout the two thousand years of Orthodox Church life will reveal a continuity that would simply be impossible without divine involvement. It's not absolutely perfect in every writing by every saint, but the overall image is quite consistent.

Holy Tradition is not a construction of fallible human beings. It is divinely revealed truth. It is the faith "once for all delivered to the saints" spoken of in Jude 3. Orthodox Christians hold fast to that tradition, or they are not following the Orthodox faith. Orthodox Christians do not pick and choose which parts of the rule of faith we like and which we do not. We are of course free to reject the faith and leave Orthodoxy, but we should understand that's what we're doing when we choose our own path. Holy Tradition cannot be altered according to our tastes, since the faith has its origins not in man, but in God. It is nevertheless lived through man, primarily through the God-man Jesus Christ, but secondarily through all who participate in Him in the Church.

Although my life in the Church is quite far from perfect, the life of the Church *as the Church*, expressed in the Scriptures and in all of Holy Tradition, is always perfect, because Christ is the Church's chief member and Head. And in Him, the life of the Church is not only perfect but eternal, existing from before all time in the divine communion of the Son with the Father and the Holy Spirit. And grafted into Him are imperfect people who struggle to live up to the fullness of the apostolic faith, to be united to the Holy Trinity in Christ.

The Church doesn't exist only to answer the questions, "Who's in charge here?" or "Whom can we trust?" as though it were simply an organization that mediated authority. But authority is one element of what it means to come together as people who are being incorporated into Christ. We have to receive the truth from somewhere, and that means we have to trust. Orthodox Christianity says you can trust the Orthodox Church not because it is made up of an external group of powerful people given authority over everyone else, nor because it has a perfect method for externally interpreting the Bible, but because it is organically the same community established by Christ, who remains the chief member of the Church, giving it its authority internally.

For the Orthodox, being outside the Orthodox Church and its expression of authority does not mean one has no possibility of connecting with God, nor does the Church even teach that being outside of any Christian faith means that. It's not about whose "team" is the best. The reason we believe there is a right way to do these things is that we believe Orthodoxy represents the fullest, most authentic expression of the Christian faith. And we believe that because Orthodoxy is consistent with what the first Christians taught and practiced, and also because the Orthodox community is actually descended from that first community. We believe we are in the right place, believing the right things and doing the right things; but the point of that belief is not to enable us to go on a rant about how everyone else is wrong and Orthodoxy is right. Rather, these things are means to an end, and that end is knowing God. And we believe that God revealed how we can know Him best.

Doing the right things is part of the basic fabric of any knowledge of God, and so we now turn to our final chapter, which is on the Christian mystery of morality.

CHAPTER FIVE

The Mystery of Morality

Why Be Moral?

Virtue exists for truth; but truth does not exist for virtue.

St. Maximus the Confessor, *Ambigua* 90

THE ETHICS OF SANTA CLAUS
AND THE ETHICS OF CHRIST

For many, the notion of who the Christians' God is and what our moral action regarding Him ought to be is essentially summarized in the lyrics to "Santa Claus Is Coming to Town": "He knows if you've been bad or good, so be good for goodness' sake!" God is portrayed as an arbitrary Judge who has set up certain rules and will zap you if you disobey them. If you get "saved," then God will not zap you. Yet being "saved" is a raw deal compared with what's at stake with the arrangement made with Santa Claus—Santa will give you presents if you're good, but God only saves you from Himself. Heaven might not be a bad place to live forever, though what we've heard about it might sound kind of boring.

For many people who believe in this theology or who have been hurt by it, Christian ethics do not fundamentally have anything to do with the core content of the Christian faith. There is no connection between the doctrines of the Holy Trinity and the Incarnation and the way we ought to live. Thus, for those who emphasize ethics, those who stress doctrine are "out of touch," while those who emphasize doctrine look upon those who stress ethics as traitors to central Christian truths. For the doctrine-focused believers, what is important is that you believe certain things; how you live doesn't matter as much. Those for whom faith is mainly a system of ethics regard doctrine as being unimportant—what's important is that you live a "good life."

And then there are skeptical people who reject both sides of this dichotomy, seeing both Christian ethics and Christian doctrine as irrelevant to real life. In our own time, this rejection is becoming more and more common. Many people simply cannot see why they shouldn't do whatever they want to do. If it feels good to me, and especially if it doesn't seem to be hurting anyone else, why shouldn't I do it?

For the Orthodox Christian, neither of these approaches to Christian theology and ethics will work, and so, like the skeptic, the Orthodox reject the dichotomy. When we preach that God is a Trinity of three divine Persons, that proclamation has everything to do with how we live. When we affirm the Incarnation of the God-man Jesus Christ, that means our morality is shaped in certain ways. Likewise, the way we live affects not just our eternal status in heaven or hell after we die and are resurrected, but it shapes our experience of God in this life as well.

Orthodox Christianity does not preach an essentially "legal" system of ethics, in which you are "in" or "out" of heaven or the Church based on doing something "good" or "bad." Rather, our whole moral tradition is based on our experience of real life, asking such questions as: Who am I? Who is God? What does it mean to be human? What does it mean to be Christ? How can I be united with God? What is the relationship between man and creation? For Orthodoxy, morality is applied theology, and it goes beyond ethics. It's not just a list of things you should or shouldn't do, either. It's a whole way of life—communion with God.

THE DOGMATIC FOUNDATION OF ORTHODOX MORALITY

Before we get deeper into Orthodox Christian morality, both on the personal level and on the level that touches on public life, let's recall the two central dogmas of the Orthodox faith: the Trinity and the Incarnation. These two dogmas and everything that flows from them are what determine the whole life of the Orthodox Christian. They determine our morality, our belief in the sacraments, our ascetical tradition, our ecclesiology, our understanding of ordained ministry, our beliefs about who mankind is—in short, all our theology and religious practice. If we do not immerse ourselves in the reality described by these two dogmas, then we are not Orthodox Christians.

God is the Holy Trinity—the Father, the Son, and the Holy Spirit, three Persons in one divine Essence. There are two kinds of attributes pertaining to God—things common to the divine nature, and things pertaining only to one Person. Thus, attributes like divinity, eternality, perfection, holiness, and so forth are common to all three Persons, while attributes like fatherhood or sonship are unique to only one Person. God is a perfect community of three Persons, a communion united in perfect love.

Jesus Christ is the incarnate Son of God. He who existed before all the ages and shared with the Father all that it means to be God stepped into history and became human. He became human in every sense, though without committing any sins. He was and is a real, particular, touchable physical human man. He is fully God and fully man, one Person in two natures.

These two dogmas set the framework for Orthodox moral theology. Because God Himself is a communion of Persons, and because we are made according to His image, we too were made to live in communion, both with God and with each other. Because Christ is the incarnate God-man, truly human in every way, our participation in Him (which is what salvation actually is) will also involve every aspect of what it means to be human, both materially and immaterially, for both our souls and our bodies.

The Scriptures record that when God conceived of man, He purposed to make Him "according to Our image" (Gen. 1:26). This is the wording in the Septuagint, the official Old Testament of the Orthodox Church. The Septuagint uses "according to Our image" and not "in Our image." Mankind is not the image of God, but made according to that image, like an ink picture made with a rubber stamp. The image of the invisible God is Jesus Christ (Col. 1:15). Thus, we were made according to Christ. He is our template. He is our standard. It is Jesus Christ who is imprinted on every human person from the moment of conception.

What this means is that the way we live our lives—not only in terms of what we might think of as "moral acts," but everything—relates to our original creation as human persons. Our proper destiny chosen before our creation was that we would be like Christ, that we would be by grace what He is by nature. And as we mentioned briefly in chapter two, grace is the uncreated energies of God, His actual presence in this world. Grace *is* God.

By nature, Christ is both God and man. By grace (God's presence in us), we can become human beings filled up with

God, in such deep communion with Him that people see God when they look at us, that we begin to gain the attributes of God. Christ represents the perfect union of God and man by who He is, while we can participate in that same union by becoming more like Him, by communing with Him. Since we have free will, we can choose to walk a path different from the one leading to the destiny our Creator designed for us. But if we choose to walk that path of destiny and stay on it, then we will become truly human.

Thus, we find the purpose of everything it means to be an Orthodox Christian, whether it is our participation in the sacraments, which are physical means by which we touch God directly; or our ascetical life of fasting, almsgiving, chastity, and modesty in possessions; or simply obeying the commandments of God not to transgress against our created nature or against the created nature of other persons or any part of creation. Orthodox Christian morality is therefore not mere adherence to a list of ethical commands. Rather, morality is the life in total freedom of the person who is acting according to his nature as God created it. Knowing who God truly is and becoming like Him requires a moral life. Christ said, "Blessed are the pure in heart, for they shall see God" (Matt. 5:8). And since knowing God is the content of eternal life (John 17:3), purity is necessary for salvation.

THE FREEDOM OF MORALITY:
BECOMING ALL FLAME

It may strike us as odd to say that morality is actually freedom, since we usually think of morality as being something
that limits us. For the young man who wants to get drunk
or have sex with his girlfriend, morality doesn't sound like
freedom at all. But his understanding of morality is probably
in terms of the ethics of Santa Claus. He won't get presents
at Christmas if he goes ahead with his immoral plans. So
what? He would rather enjoy the buzz and the sexual rush
or even just the feeling of emotional and physical intimacy
than get presents. And whom is he hurting, anyway? How
does being moral actually do anything? Heaven is a long way
off, just like Christmas, and it's not really so enticing that
it isn't worth trading for what feels good and is available to
him right now. Or, even if he does have a sense of morality
that he's trying to follow, he may be playing a game with
himself as to just how far he'll go without crossing the line.

In these and other moments of ethical decision, those
who follow the culturally popular theology of good and evil
see no inherent connection between ethics and doctrine.
For our hypothetical young man and his girlfriend, what
does it matter if the God of the universe is a Trinity of three
divine Persons or that Christ is the incarnate God-man?
Who cares? What does that have to do with "real life"? What

bearing does that have on how they feel about each other and how good it feels to sleep together?

For Orthodox Christians to affirm that a moral life is a life of freedom and not restriction, we first have to ask what freedom is. In secular life, *freedom* is usually defined as "getting to do whatever I want." In other words, freedom is associated with permission and even approval. Orthodox theology, however, teaches that freedom is instead about energy and power. When a man is truly set free, he now has powers and abilities that he did not previously possess. In the lives of Orthodox saints (the people we believe successfully lived Christian life with total authenticity), there are many examples of this truth. The saints not only did things like speak with angels, but they healed the sick, raised the dead, saw into the future, teleported, looked into people's hearts, and accomplished what may be the most miraculous feat of all: they loved their enemies.

Our freedom as Orthodox Christians is not freedom from any limitations, but rather freedom to be truly human, to act according to the awesome potential with which God created us. We do become free *from* something, and that is sin. Sin is a weight that pulls us down, a disease that saps our strength and cripples us, making us incapable of truly living. But we also become free *for* something. The moral life is not just about regaining health, but about gaining new strength to accomplish true wonders.

Therefore, the moral person is not one who merely obeys

arbitrary rules. He is the athlete who knows what it takes to fly down the racetrack. He knows he will eat a certain diet, push himself every day, take the right medicines, and shun certain kinds of behaviors. If he doesn't do this, he won't have the energy and power to run the race. He will not be free to fly but will instead be trapped by his transient desires. And giving in to them can wreck all the preparation he's done. The thrill of the moment can supplant the work of a lifetime.

A brief story is told in the *Sayings of the Desert Fathers* (an ancient text about the lives of Christians in the deserts of Egypt):

> *Abba Lot went to see Abba Joseph and said to him, "Abba, as far as I can, I say my [daily prayers], I fast a little, I pray and meditate. I live in peace as far as I can. I purify my thoughts. What else can I do?"*
>
> *Then the old man stood up, stretched his arms towards heaven. His fingers became like ten lamps of fire and he said to him, "If you want, you can be all flame."*[18]

This is what morality has to do with doctrine. If we believe we can become "all flame," that we can have a degree of communion with God that will amaze even the angels, that our lives can be so transformed that we're not just "good" but actually holy, that we can experience the fire of the presence of God with such intensity that doubts about His existence could never enter us again—then it is only natural that we should ask, "How can I have this?"

THE PURPOSE OF MORALITY: KNOWING JESUS CHRIST

If more people heard that this is what the Gospel actually involves—not merely "getting out of hell" or "being good," but a true intimacy with the God who is closer to us than we are to ourselves—and if Christian preachers verified that preaching with authentic attempts to live the life, we can scarcely imagine what the impact would be. Certainly, we would still experience the temptations of living only for the moment, but we would have declared war against the infectious disease of corruption that ravages each of us from the moment of our entrance into this fallen world. And in that declaration of war, we would have raised a banner that is worth flocking to.

Orthodox morality does not consist merely of following rules or inching up close to some arbitrary line we won't cross. Rather, for the Orthodox Christian, morality is inherently relational and focused on a goal. It's not a question of which lines we cannot cross, but rather of what our whole direction in life is. What is the vector of our souls? Are we aimed toward intimacy and intense communion with God in Christ, or are we aimed in another direction? If it is the latter, it won't matter which lines we cross or which we don't.

Dancing perilously close to some razor-thin line between morality and immorality is not what it means to be moral from the Orthodox standpoint. Such an approach reminds

me of the kid who puts his fingers right next to his sister's
face and gleefully announces, "I'm not touching you! I'm
not touching you!" It's possible in this life to appear to be
"moral" in terms of following rules and yet still be steering
your soul in the wrong direction. By the same token, a fre-
quent sinner who nevertheless sincerely and deeply repents
will be welcomed into the Kingdom of heaven, and in the
purity of his heart, he will see God.

St. Maximus the Confessor put the proposition this way:
"Virtue exists for truth; but truth does not exist for virtue."
It is critical that we understand this saying. Virtue—that
is, morality—is not the purpose of all our dogma and our
church life. We do not become Christians in order to become
moral people. Christ did not come to this Earth in order to
make bad people good. He came in order to make dead people live. And that is only accomplished by participation in
the Truth, that is, in Jesus Christ Himself, who is the Truth
(John 14:6).

Morality has a purpose beyond simply ordering us into
a stable and polite society. Orthodox Christians need to
understand this well, know this purpose, and be able to
explain it to our children, our friends, our families, and all
those whose lives we participate in. Why? Because morality
is perceived more and more as irrelevant, because people are
failing to see any point in it, because the ethical teachings
of popular Christianity fail to reveal any deeper purpose. I
don't think most people who live immorally do so because

they're deliberately trying to rebel. I think most of them do it because they just don't see the point of living otherwise. And when there is no apparent purpose to ethics, we resort to relativism (the belief that there is no absolute truth). After all, if morality is just a social construct or adherence to some arbitrary set of rules, why should your morality trump mine? Whose morality?

Most of us are willing to put restraints on ourselves if we believe it serves a greater purpose. Consider the willingness of many people to change their eating or exercise habits for health purposes. Consider how people sacrifice to provide for their children, to gain a position, or to achieve some goal. Likewise, morality from the Orthodox point of view really does have a purpose.

One might suspect this means we teach "situational" or purely "utilitarian" ethics, because it seems morality exists only to serve some purpose, rather than for its own sake. But should morality really exist for its own sake? For one thing, morality for its own sake has failed to inspire a moral culture. But even aside from that, we have to ask this question: What makes something good? What makes something moral? Is it because a particular behavior is congruent with an arbitrary list of rules? Who says those rules are the right ones?

Christian morality comes from God. He has defined what it means to be moral. Christian moral tradition is part of the revelation given by God. But are His moral precepts arbitrary? Are they just what He happens to like? Or is the morality He has given us driven by some deeper purpose? Yes, it is.

There are at least fifteen places in the Bible in which keeping God's commandments is directly connected with loving God. The most direct of these is in John 14:15, where Christ says, "If you love Me, keep My commandments." We can thus conclude that those who love God will keep His commandments. The contrapositive is also true: If we do not keep His commandments, then we do not love Him. And if we do not love God, how can we hope for eternal salvation, which is being in communion with God? Why would we even want it?

Even aside from morality being a proof of our love of God, Christ has more to say in John 14:21: "He who has My commandments and keeps them, it is he who loves Me. And he who loves Me will be loved by My Father, and I will love him and manifest Myself to him." In other words, if we act according to the morality God has given to us, we are not only made capable of receiving God's love in Christ, but we are also made capable of receiving His manifestation of Himself to us. This is the same as "Blessed are the pure in heart, for they shall see God" (Matt. 5:8).

Jesus says in John 15:10, "If you keep My commandments, you will abide in My love, just as I have kept My Father's commandments and abide in His love." Keeping the commandments of Christ is therefore not only identified with loving God and receiving love from God in the right way, but it is also identified with the very life of Christ Himself. Jesus keeps the Father's commandments and abides in His love, and we can therefore do the same. That is, when we keep God's commandments, we are entering into the very life of the Holy Trinity. Orthodox morality is not only ethical but mystical.

Orthodox morality has a goal. Moral actions are not good *in themselves*, because goodness is not an independent attribute. Goodness is good because it has reference to God, not because you or I say it's good or because there is an isolated "good" quality that goodness has. Something is good only when it exists according to the way God intended it when He created it to exist. Morality is therefore part of the path to the love and knowledge of God. Morality is part of how we can be united to God, how we can enter into the divine life of the Father, Son, and Holy Spirit.

ASCETICISM: THE SHAPE OF MORALITY

One of the key elements of Orthodox Christian life which makes it so distinct from the other forms of Christianity is asceticism. For most Protestant Christians, asceticism is almost entirely unheard of, while for Roman Catholics, it is either a sort of footnote or something mainly associated with monasticism. But for Orthodox Christians, asceticism is the basic shape of the moral life for everyone who is part of the Church.

So what does *asceticism* mean? What does it mean for

Orthodox Christians to be ascetics? Is this something expected of everyone, or just a handful, most especially monks and nuns? Asceticism—or *askesis*—is expected of all Orthodox Christians, so let's try to understand what it means and what its significance is for the spiritual life of seeking to be introduced to and to meet God.

It is a fundamental element of Orthodox understanding of humanity's predicament in a fallen world that our attachment to created matter—physical stuff—dominates us. We like food. We like physical pleasure. We like possessions. We seek these things above almost everything else. That is not how God created humanity. God created humanity so that the body and all matter would be in harmony with the spirit, directed by it as a brain directs the body. When disharmony between these elements occurs, there is sickness—both physical and spiritual—within the person, and on the cosmic scale between persons and the whole created order. The purpose of asceticism is to reassert the proper order, to train the human person not to be attached to and dominated by created things but rather to put them into their proper perspective and context.

The word *askesis,* though it originally referred to athletic training, is the Greek term for the ascetical life, a life of freedom in choosing to set aside pleasures of the created world, choosing to act with an attitude of gentle restraint, in order to refocus one's energies on God, who is uncreated. We might thus be tempted to see asceticism as dualistic, a rejection of the physical world in favor of the spiritual world, and certain kinds of non-Orthodox or non-Christian ascetical religious practices and doctrines are indeed guilty of this charge. But Orthodox Christian asceticism's purpose is not to denigrate material reality, but rather to restore it to its proper place so that it might reveal its true purpose as a vehicle for divine sanctification.

We as human beings (especially those in American culture) are dominated by our appetites. It is no secret that our appetites are largely responsible for most environmental harm that occurs today. Our appetites are also at the heart of most of our societal and personal afflictions, including murder, theft, divorce, hatred, war, drunkenness, abortion, greed, sexual disorderliness, and so on. But we do not usually address the root cause of this harm. Rather, we attempt to come up with artificial systems to fix its symptoms and effects, all the while not seeking the cure of the inner malady. Orthodoxy's cure for this malady is asceticism.

Imagine for a moment if every person in your country were to turn from the culture of consumption and instead embrace simplicity. It is a curious thing that in the Gospels, Jesus urges His followers humbly to lay aside possessions and the drive to consume (often mentioning how misuse of wealth can get in the way of spiritual life), yet some ostensibly "Christian" countries are cultures of possession and consumption, always demanding "rights" rather than practicing humility. If we all embraced asceticism even at a very modest level, a massive economic bomb would drop. But when the fallout from that bomb cleared away, what would be left would be people ready to use their hands, hearts, and minds for something other than eating up the natural world and each other. As St. Basil the Great once said, "Consider that not everything is made for our bellies."

If we all fasted from meat and other animal products the way Orthodox practice prescribes, roughly half the days of the year, the food industry would be transformed. If we all abstained from sexual activity entirely outside of marriage, and within marriage for certain periods, the birth control industry would become largely irrelevant. And certainly, these practices would radically alter our health care industry, probably rendering much political debate almost meaningless. And consider if people traded massive houses and cars for something much more commensurate with their needs. Whether you believe in manmade global warming or not, we would be looking at a whole new context regarding carbon footprints, energy independence, "green" energy, and so on.

The primary purpose of Orthodox Christian asceticism is training for the art of prayer. Yet in drawing close to God by using asceticism, the Christian draws the creation with him, bringing himself more and more into harmony with it. He becomes less disruptive and far more ready to work together with the land and with his fellow human persons to prosper a more restrained, yet ultimately fuller and more humane civilization. Orthodoxy bears within its theology the affirmation that this created world, including the human body, was created as *good* by God *and remains good*, although in a distorted state. Therefore, the ascetical, moral life takes created matter into account, realizing that there is no morality without a proper attitude toward all creatures, whether human or otherwise. This attitude includes not only respect and restraint but ultimately deep, self-sacrificial love.

Asceticism is therefore the actual shape of the morality of Orthodox Christians. Asceticism is not about individual achievement in piety, but about communal life with one another and with the world. Therefore, whenever we live in an ascetical way, we will be loving one another. The ascetic does not take from others. He treads lightly upon the Earth and among his fellow human beings, giving to them from whatever he has. The true philanthropist is the ascetic. The true humanitarian is the ascetic. The true environmentalist is the ascetic. The true hero is the ascetic. The true artist is the ascetic.

Ascetical life is characterized by restraint, by not violating the freedom of the other, by not exploiting the other, by sacrificing for the other. The proper use of created things and the proper attitude of humility toward others is, in theological terms, called *chastity*. We may usually think of chastity in sexual terms, but it can be much broader. It is living so that we conform to our nature as God created it. It is not so much an attitude of denial as of proper organization, of using human energies as God created them to be used. Chastity is the redirection of misdirected energies, correcting them so that they are not destructive, but healing and creative.

With this one essential posture toward our fellow human persons and toward all creation, it is almost easy to see how morality works itself out. How could a truly chaste person ever lie, cheat, steal, fornicate, exploit, envy, be lazy, or become angry with someone? How could our hypothetical young man mentioned above draw his girlfriend into sin, knowing that doing so is a denial of their true created nature, which includes sexual chastity? How could such a person ever consider taking the life of an innocent unborn child, whether out of expedience, fear, or desperation? When we perceive the inner holiness and immense worth of everything, we begin to treat it all differently.

It is our ability to say *no* to the demands of our appetites, to exercise restraint in the service of greater, nobler desires that separates us from the beasts. It is our power to direct our desires toward the uncreated God rather than toward the necessities and transience of created things that ennobles us, revealing us truly as sons and daughters of God.

MORALITY AND THE CULTURE WARS

In discussing Orthodox Christian moral theology, there is one theological principle we always have to make explicit. In Orthodox soteriology—our theology of salvation—we believe that man's free will is a critical element in his spiritual transformation. No one can be forced into communion with God. Ostensibly "moral" acts that are committed under duress are not truly moral.

While God always chooses man, man must choose God for himself and act on that choice in order for the relationship to work. God will never force communion on anyone, and if we are going to behave in an Orthodox manner, we cannot try to force it on anyone else, either.

Morality is therefore not primarily about specific external acts but about the attitude of the heart. If the heart is not attuned to living the ascetical, chaste life of the Christian seeking to know God and to love Him, then adherence to external rules of moral living will be fruitless.

Humility is a critical element in our salvation, both in our communion with God and in our communion with other people. In practical terms, this means that if we want to be transformed by God, we can't do it on our own terms. Our acceptance of God's proposal must be voluntary, but we must accept it. We cannot dictate the terms of our salvation.

We also cannot dictate the terms of someone else's salvation. No matter what someone else's temptation or sin is, if we lay down judgment on that person—including forcing him out of the community, shunning him, or speaking evil of him—then we ourselves have departed from the path of salvation. If we compare ourselves to others, then we should always come away with the conclusion that, should we make it into the Kingdom, we will go in last. I am the worst of sinners (1 Tim. 1:15). I may not have the particular sin I see in my brother, but my sins collectively are much worse. My brother may be repenting, but I am not. I am usurping Christ's place if I judge him.

All that being said, there are some things we can say regarding the place of Orthodox Christian morality in our modern culture. Orthodox Christians do have a stake in what are commonly called the "culture wars." The Orthodox have a duty to speak the truth prophetically to the culture, to engage with the world around us, not so that we can feel better about our own supposed morality, because we are sinners, but so that the world can hear the Gospel. The world needs to hear about how to love God and keep His commandments, so that everyone and the whole creation may be brought back into harmony with God and may receive the divine life. If we do not bring the message of God's design for the world, then we do not love the world.

There are some who say Christians should not make any active engagement with the culture, that we should retreat into our communities, try to live holy lives, and then welcome people who show up at our doorsteps. Not every Christian thinks this, but many do. This was not, however, the approach of the prophets, Jesus Christ, His apostles, or the saints who followed them. None of them had any compunction about engaging the moral issues of their time in public places. They preached the Gospel by including strong words not in condemnation, but rather in pointing the way to communion with God—speaking truth to power, but with love. True holiness for the Orthodox means engagement, because we are commanded to work for the salvation of the world, to baptize every person in the Name of the Father, the Son, and the Holy Spirit, teaching them to observe all that Christ commanded us (Matt. 28:19–20).

That said, there are two fronts on which Orthodox Christians can be active in terms of the culture wars. The first is in the culture directly, in seeking to affect the lives of those around us, remembering that the Lord's command was not "love the masses," but rather "love your neighbor." Our first duty is not only to demonstrate what a truly moral life looks like, but to teach this life to others. It also means we work directly to ease the suffering of others, even if we disapprove of their behavior or lifestyle or recognize it as genuinely harmful. We also work to bring others to understand the Orthodox Christian viewpoint through persuasion and active love.

The second front is the political front. This front is more indirect in terms of its ability to effect salvation. Our first duty is to transform the culture directly. If we do that, then politics will naturally follow. That being said, there are some things we can seek to accomplish politically, if at all possible, even if the transformation of the culture is not yet complete. We don't find much in the way of worked-out political theory in the Bible or in the writings of the Church Fathers, but there is at least one clear duty that government should be performing: the restraining of evildoers, particularly those who constitute a public menace, so that we may establish peace.

This does not mean every immoral act should also be illegal, but it does mean some immoral acts are such a clear threat to society that the government has a duty to restrain those who commit them. We cannot, as the cliché goes, "legislate morality." We cannot pass laws that make people moral, precisely because morality is an ascetical attitude of the heart. But we can restrain public evil in order to establish peace. We have a duty to defend the innocent, to foster an environment in which people can seek God and find Him.

There are some who might say we have no business attempting to affect the political process in terms of Christian faith, that doing so constitutes "imposing our religion" on others and thus violates the freedom Orthodox theology teaches. But the Orthodox Church has never condoned absolute freedom in the *secular* sense, people being "allowed" to do just anything they want to. Some actions really do constitute a public menace. There is a difference between the freedom that is the power to be holy and the so-called "freedom" that is the license to commit any act we desire.

Likewise, at least for those who live in countries that have a tradition of representative government, we should understand that this tradition has certain foundational principles that have no basis in purely secular or scientific philosophy.

One is the affirmation in the American Declaration of Independence that every person is created equal and endowed by the Creator with unalienable rights. Yet logic and experience tell us that people are not equal. Some people are smarter or stronger than others. Some people contribute more to society than others. So on what basis do we call them "equal"? It is only in transcendent terms that we are equal. Intrinsic human worth is not something that can be recognized on purely secular terms; it is the result of endowment by the Creator.

Most basic political affirmations have a transcendent origin, placing value on human life not for utilitarian or meritocratic purposes, but simply because it is human. This principle cannot be derived from pure science, which in itself places no more value on the collection of elements that makes up a human person than on the collection that makes up a rock. Why should life have more value than non-life? And why should human life have more value than plant or animal life? The answer to those questions is found in transcendent principles, most of which have their origins in religion. That this is true means not that religion is being "imposed" on anyone, but that even non-believers enjoy the benefits of religion without being forced to adopt it.

Further, democratic political tradition says we can choose to elect representatives based on whatever motivations we like. Ballots don't ask *why*. To expect that, for instance, a religious believer should leave his beliefs at the door when going into a voting booth is just as ridiculous as to expect that the capitalist or socialist should do so. When we consider that many candidates are elected primarily because of how they look on television, why should anyone object if a voter makes his choices based in his most deeply held beliefs?

In any event, whatever we may do, Orthodox Christians try to remember that our engagement with the world is not for our own selfish gain, not to "recruit" people to our way of thinking, to get them to join our philosophical "club." Rather, it has only one purpose: the salvation of ourselves and of the world. All of our interaction with this world should be for its salvation.

In our own time, our engagement on these two fronts—the cultural and the political—seems mainly to be centered in one major question: What does it mean to be human? The Orthodox Christian faith has a clear answer to this question: We are the children of God, created according to His image—created according to Christ—and made for communion with Him. This question and its answer inform all the paramount moral issues of our time.

MORALITY AS LITURGY

It is part of the genius of Orthodox Christian theology—that is, its particular, unique manner of operation—to affirm that created matter is critical in our salvation. We saw in chapter three how created matter finds its height and perfection in the Eucharist and in all liturgical worship. If we consider that Orthodox ascetical, moral life is by its nature liturgical, then we may perhaps understand it better.

As we have said, morality is not really about adherence to a list of rules but rather about the proper attitude of the heart, a certain lightly treading restraint. The ascetic walks through this world with reverence and love for it and all that is in it because he sees God dwelling in all of it, because working to realign his created nature according to its created design brings him into union with God. Orthodox Christian liturgical worship is therefore the ultimate expression of this ascetical attitude toward the world.

Consider the worshiper in the Divine Liturgy, the eucharistic worship service. He enters the church with humility, reverence, care, and awe. He venerates the holiness he sees around him with acts of respect and love. He helps to maintain the order of the worship event by not disturbing others, by helping others to do the same. He listens carefully to the Scriptures and the sermon so that he can find out what is in himself that still needs repentance. He puts himself last. He receives into himself all the joy and wonder of the glory of God, which is the presence of God Himself. He receives the Holy Eucharist, not gobbling it or pushing his way to get it, but carefully, reverently, and with thankfulness to God. He is not driven by his appetites, but only by his desire to know and to love God, to become one with Him and with those praying with him.

In this image of the worshiper, we see the human person at her finest, at her most human. She is in harmony with her fellow man, with all creation, and most especially with her God. She is doing what she was created to do. Is it any wonder, then, that we see that those in the Church who are most dedicated to worship also are most dedicated to the moral life? It is because worship forms the moral person, an ascetic who, in chastity and with restraint, engages herself, those around her, and the whole world with love and self-sacrifice. The moral person refers her every action back to God, revealing the mystical purpose of Orthodox Christian morality.

CONCLUSION

Encountering the Divine

In asking all these questions, in entering into these mysteries, I have attempted to sketch a little bit of sacred space—or perhaps to clear out some space—in which we might encounter the divine, in which we might be introduced to God. Yet just because we draw the circle or clear out the obstacles from the circle does not mean we have stepped into it, nor does it mean God has chosen to step into it. Just like us, He is free not to show up. He doesn't have to come when we call, even if we do call in the right way, with humility.

But it is right for us to hope that, if we can learn to call upon God in the right way, by making ourselves available to Him in humility, then we can have that encounter. If we step into the circle ready to meet God, then we can reasonably hope He will make that introduction happen.

From His point of view, He's been waiting in the circle for us to join Him there. But we have to call upon Him well and be present to Him and for Him. What you bring to any encounter will have a profound effect on what happens in it, and we're talking here about an encounter with God. So what should we bring? How do we enter?

If you ever happen to be present at mealtime at my house, you may hear the voices of small people making various requests, whether it is for access to papa's doughnut, to be released from the high chair, to be exempted from what everyone else is eating, and so forth. How those requests are answered depends very much on the manner in which the request is made.

The same holds true for so much in life—if we want something, we have to know how to ask for it or how to look for it. How much more is this true for the presence of the mysterious God? We cannot simply turn around in a circle, announce that we have not seen God, and thus declare Him not to exist. We have to know how to look for Him, how to ask for His presence.

Near the beginning of this book, we mentioned the book *Beginning to Pray* by Metropolitan Anthony Bloom. In it, Metropolitan Anthony addresses this question of how we prepare for God's presence. Often, when we desire for God to make an appearance, it is because we want something from Him. We usually have no sense of *relationship* when we lay out our expectations of God. We may respectfully ask what we desire from Him, but if all we ever do with Him is to make claims on His providence, are we seeking to overcome the separation, that sense of absence? Are we really seeking an introduction to God, or are we just seeking something *from* Him?

We may complain that God does not answer our prayers, that He does not come when we call, but, as Metropolitan Anthony writes:

> *If you look at the relationship in terms of mutual relationship, you will see that God could complain about us a great deal more than we about Him. We complain that He does not make Himself present to us for the few minutes we reserve for Him, but what about the twenty-three and a half hours during which God may be knocking at our door and we answer 'I am busy, I am sorry' or when we do not answer at all because we do not even hear the knock at the door of our heart, of our minds, of our conscience, of our life. So there is a situation in which we have no right to complain of the absence of God, because we are a great deal more absent than He ever is.*[19]

I would like to introduce here a little more Jewish philosophical wisdom, because sometimes words from outside my tradition can help me to understand it better. The nineteenth-century Polish Hasidic rabbi Menachem Mendel Morgensztern of Kotzk, better known as "the Kotzker Rebbe," once asked his students, "Where is God?"

They replied, "Does not the Bible tell us that the whole world is full of His glory?"

He responded, "That may be fine for the heavenly angels,

but the answer for man is different. God is present wherever human beings allow God to enter."[20]

It is kind of a scandalous thing to say, but this is what Christians say about the ultimate entrance of God into this world, His revelation as a man—He entered because one of us allowed Him to enter. We believe He entered into humanity at the permission of a first-century Jewish virgin.

The Creator of the universe Himself stepped into our world, our time, onto our planet, into our humanity, by being conceived of the Holy Spirit at the consent of the Virgin Mary. He entered into human experience in that most intimate, secret, and sacred of human places—the womb of a virgin. That is the kind of closeness and intimacy He desires with us.

But we must also remember that while God is both giving and faithful (not to mention relentless), He is also free. He is free not to show up when we call. And more than that, we have to know what gift He offers when He does show up, which is *Himself.* As Jesus said, eternal life is to know God.

Metropolitan Anthony puts it this way:

> We should be aware that He cannot come to us [when] we are not there to receive Him. We want something from Him, not Him at all. Is that a relationship? Do we behave that way with our friends? Do we aim at what friendship can give us or is it the friend whom we love? Is this true with regard to the Lord?[21]

God has come to you by becoming a human person like you, and He has come to you precisely for *you*, not for anything

He can get from you. He needs nothing from you. He is here because it's you. Are you here because it's Him?

As we complete this meditation on how we can be introduced to God, I would like to close with some words from St. Symeon the New Theologian, a Christian monk who lived roughly a thousand years ago. In Symeon's time, there were Christians who claimed that encounters with God were impossible in this life, that we should study God and then wait until the next life for a true introduction. Symeon forcefully insisted that this teaching was false, as he himself had had numerous mystical experiences of God. Here is what he wrote about one of them:

> *I wander and I am on fire, searching here and there,*
> *and nowhere do I find the Lover of my soul.*
> *I frequently cast glances all around to see my Beloved*
> *and He, the invisible One, never shows Himself to me.*
> *But when I begin to weep, as desperate, then*
> *He shows Himself and He looks at me, He who contemplates all*
>   *creatures.*
> *In amazement, I admire the splendor of His beauty,*
> *and how, having opened the heavens, the Creator inclined*
> *and showed me His glory, indescribable, marvellous.*
> *And so who would draw nearer to Him?*
> *Or how would he be carried away toward measureless heights?*
> *While I reflect on this, He Himself is discovered within myself,*
> *resplendent in the interior of my miserable heart,*
> *illuminating me on all sides with His immortal splendor*
> *completely intertwined with me, He embraces me totally.*
> *He gives Himself to me, the unworthy one,*
> *And I am filled with His love and His beauty,*

and I am sated with divine delight and sweetness.
I share in the light, I participate also in the glory,
and my face shines like my Beloved's,
and all my members become bearers of light.[22]

So if you're not having supernatural, miraculous, mystical experiences of God's presence, does that mean you don't know Him, that you've never really been introduced to Him? No, it doesn't mean that. But is there a test? Is there some way to know you're actually connecting with God?

If someone shows up at church looking to "get something out of it," or if he spends his time in prayer only asking for things, or if he has a sense that God owes him something because of his faithful service to Him, that he should be getting more credit for what he does "for God" or "for the Church," then I gently suggest that he is not spending time with God, but only with his own ego. God is present with him, but he's not connecting with God, because he's not present to Him and for Him. He's just present to himself and for himself.

It really is simple. Consider someone you love. You love being with that person. You love his presence. You're not there to get anything from him. You're there to be with him. And you come away from the experience more at peace with yourself and with the world, knowing there is meaning and purpose in life. You are at home. And over time, you find that you become something like that person.

If that is your experience when it comes to God, then,

yes, you have been introduced to Him and are meeting Him and getting to know Him. And if participation in the life of beloved friends or family changes you for the good, bringing you closer to them and making you more like them, consider what participation in God means.

As St. Symeon wrote, "I share in the light, I participate also in the glory, / and my face shines like my Beloved's, / and all my members become bearers of light."

May it be so for each of us.

An Annotated Bibliography

Author's Note: The following is a collection of titles that are recommended for the newcomer to Orthodox Christianity. Their bibliographical information is included, along with some remarks commending them to the reader. This is by no means an exhaustive list, but the works were selected because each opens a unique introductory door into the experience of the Orthodox Christian faith.

As of this writing, there is not much published in English introducing Orthodox Christianity specifically to non-Christian readers. Thus, many of these works assume some knowledge of Christianity. They should still be fairly accessible to the non-Christian reader, however. Some are more advanced in style than others.[§]

[§]   Many of these works are available at store.ancientfaith.com.

GENERAL AND BASIC WORKS ON ORTHODOXY

Clément, Olivier. *The Living God: A Catechism for the Christian Faith* (2 vol. set). St. Vladimir's Seminary Press, 1989.

Olivier Clément (1921–2009) was a French convert to Orthodoxy from agnosticism who eventually became a seminary professor in Paris. This set is his attempt to introduce families and inquirers to the core elements of the faith. It is different from older forms of catechism, which centered on dry lists of questions and answers, in that it gives a vivid presentation of the Orthodox Christian faith by using images, hymnography, and theology from the feasts and traditions of the Church.

Coniaris, Anthony M. *Introducing the Orthodox Church: Its Faith and Life*. Light & Life Publishing Company, 2007.

This book is a very basic overview of Orthodox Christianity, written in a simple style. Its purpose is catechetical and introductory. Fr. Anthony has published numerous works of this sort on many different topics, all of them quite easy to read and access.

Hopko, Thomas. *The Orthodox Faith* (4 vol. set). St. Vladimir's Seminary Press, 1972.

Commonly called "the Rainbow Series" because of its four different-colored volumes (*Doctrine, Worship, Bible and Church History,* and *Spirituality*), this basic catechetical series is written at an elementary level. It is also fully available online at: http://oca.org/orthodoxy/the-orthodox-faith

McGuckin, John Anthony. *The Orthodox Church: An Introduction to its History, Doctrine and Spiritual Culture.* Wiley-Blackwell, 2010.

Although not quite the "standard" that Timothy Ware's *The Orthodox Church* is (see below), this far more detailed work may prove to be the standard for its generation. Although it is slanted in a more academic direction, Fr. John McGuckin writes in an engaging, intelligent style that will thoroughly introduce the reader to Orthodoxy but also show its importance in the modern world, engaging Western culture in dialogue. This work also includes numerous notes, an index, a glossary of unfamiliar terms, and an extensive select bibliography.

Paul of Finland, Archbishop. *The Faith We Hold.* St. Vladimir's Seminary Press, 1999.

Archbishop Paul was the head of the Orthodox Church in Finland from 1960 to 1988, and he wrote this little book (originally in Finnish) "to describe Orthodoxy from the inside to those outside, and to offer answers to the most fundamental questions." It is an excellent and easily digestible book that can be read in just a couple of hours.

Veniaminov, Innocent. *Indication of the Way into the Kingdom of Heaven.* Holy Trinity Publications, 1999.

St. Innocent of Alaska wrote this work as a basic catechism for introducing Orthodox Christianity to the shamanistic native tribes of Alaska, whom he was sent from Russia to evangelize. The original edition was written in the nineteenth century in the Aleut language, a previously unwritten language for which St. Innocent devised an alphabet.

Ware, Kallistos. *The Orthodox Way*. St. Vladimir's Seminary Press, 1995.

First published in 1979, this is one of the most popular works introducing Orthodox Christianity. It is a brief work, organized into short chapters, each with titles like "God As Mystery," "God As Man," or "God As Prayer." It does not give a factual introduction to Orthodoxy (for that, see Ware's *The Orthodox Church*), but rather gives an introduction to the *atmosphere* of Orthodoxy—how to think and pray in Orthodox ways. The author is an English convert to Orthodoxy and now a titular metropolitan bishop who lives in Oxford.

Ware, Timothy. *The Orthodox Church*. Penguin Books, 1993.

This work is by the same author as *The Orthodox Way*, though it was written earlier—first published in 1963, before the author had become an Orthodox monk and had his name changed to Kallistos. *The Orthodox Church* is the single most popular work in English introducing Orthodox Christianity in terms of the facts of its history, beliefs, worship, and lifestyle. It is indispensable for understanding the critical encyclopedia-level knowledge about Orthodoxy.

NARRATIVE WORKS

The Book of Genesis, The Gospel of Luke, and The Acts of the Apostles.

These might seem either odd or obvious selections for this bibliography, but these three historical works in the Bible constitute most of the core narrative for understanding the Orthodox Christian faith. Genesis tells the story of how the cosmos was created and how human life began on Earth. I have selected Luke's Gospel specifically because he is most concerned with the essential details of the narrative of Jesus' earthly ministry and places it in its historical context. And Acts tells the story of the beginning of the Church's life.

Bacovcin, Helen, trans. *The Way of a Pilgrim.* Doubleday Image Books, 1992.

There are numerous translations and editions of this anonymous nineteenth-century Russian work of fiction. In it, the narrator discovers the Jesus Prayer (which has many forms, but the form used in this work is "Lord Jesus Christ, Son of God, have mercy on me, a sinner"), which opens up for him the ability to be always getting closer to God.

Bernstein, A. James. *Surprised by Christ: My Journey from Judaism to Orthodox Christianity.* Conciliar Press/Ancient Faith Publishing, 2008.

Fr. James Bernstein, the son of an Orthodox Jewish rabbi, tells the story of how he encountered Jesus Christ as the Messiah and how he came to see Him most clearly in the Orthodox Church.

Bouteneff, Vera, trans. *Father Arseny, 1893–1973: Priest, Prisoner, Spiritual Father.* St. Vladimir's Seminary Press, 1998.

Father Arseny was a prisoner in the Soviet gulags in Russia, having committed the crime of being a faithful priest in a militantly atheistic state. This nonfiction work is a series of short vignettes telling about his life in the gulags as seen by those who encountered him. A number of the stories are miraculous, and they evoke a powerful witness of faith in the midst of some of the harshest conditions mankind has ever devised. A follow-up volume, *Father Arseny: A Cloud of Witnesses* (2001), is also available, detailing the stories of many people who encountered him after his release from prison.

Farasiotis, Dionysios. *The Gurus, the Young Man, and Elder Paisios.* St. Herman of Alaska Brotherhood, 2011.

This memoir tells the story of a young Greek man who becomes deeply involved with Hindu mysticism and eventually is led back to the faith of his youth, largely through the saintly witness of Elder Paisios, a modern holy man. It describes in vivid, gripping detail his spiritual experiences, both outside Orthodoxy and within it.

Gillquist, Peter E. *Becoming Orthodox: A Journey to the Ancient Christian Faith.* Conciliar Press/Ancient Faith Publishing, 2009 (1992).

Fr. Peter Gillquist's story of how he and a group of other former evangelical Protestant leaders in Campus Crusade for Christ discovered the Orthodox faith is directed primarily toward a low-church evangelical audience. Including both narrative and commentary on doctrine and worship, it is quite easy to read and remains one of the most popular introductory works for those who have some experience with evangelicalism to learn about Orthodoxy. Gillquist helped to bring about a major evangelistic surge in Orthodoxy in the United States. He died in 2012.

Markides, Kyriacos C. *The Mountain of Silence: A Search for Orthodox Spirituality.* Random House, 2002.

The author goes on a search to understand the faith of his ancestors and encounters a modern-day holy elder in Cyprus, "Father Maximos" (a pseudonym for a real Orthodox monk), who teaches him about Orthodox spiritual life. Not everything in the author's commentary is strictly Orthodox, and he seems to be more interested in his understanding of Orthodox spirituality than the Jesus at the center of it (he says as much in one of his other works). Nevertheless, there is still much good here for the careful reader, especially in the words of Father Maximos.

Mathewes-Green, Frederica. *Facing East: A Pilgrim's Journey into the Mysteries of Orthodoxy.* HarperCollins, 2006.

Frederica Mathewes-Green, a syndicated columnist and National Public Radio commentator, and her husband, Fr. Gregory, converted to Orthodoxy from the Episcopal Church. Mathewes-Green's story is interesting in that she moved from a particularly liberal expression of Christianity (including being a convinced feminist) into Orthodoxy. She has another work, *At the Corner of East and Now* (2nd ed. Conciliar Press/Ancient Faith Publishing, 2008), which is about everyday life in the Church, along with several other books.

ORTHODOX SPIRITUALITY AND OTHER TOPICS

Bajis, Jordan. *Common Ground: An Introduction to Eastern Christianity for the American Christian.* Light & Life Publishing Company, 1989.

Common Ground is a basic, comparative book mainly aimed toward evangelicals and beginners in Orthodoxy. It has an almost workbook-like modularity and is easy to work through. Of minor note (but nonetheless worth mentioning) is that Bajis himself is not currently an Orthodox Christian. His book is still useful, however.

Bloom, Anthony. *Beginning to Pray.* Paulist Press, 1970.

This simple work by Metropolitan Anthony (Bloom) of Sourozh, the Russian Orthodox Church's bishop in London from 1962 to 2003, is probably one of the most profound and accessible works on the heart of the Christian's connection with God. It presumes little prior knowledge of Christianity and remains one of my favorite works to read again and again. It's really about what the title says it is. I had the blessing to meet Metropolitan Anthony very briefly in 2001, and his presence very much embodied the kind of beautiful simplicity in this work. All of his works are of the same style.

Cabasilas, Nicholas. *The Life in Christ.* St. Vladimir's Seminary Press, 1972.

Nicholas Cabasilas was a fourteenth-century Byzantine saint and writer. This work of devotional theology, written by a layman, is intended as a general guide to living the life in Christ. While secular humanism began to flower in the West, Cabasilas asserted that the true life of a person lies not in himself as an autonomous being, but in communion with Jesus.

Damick, Andrew Stephen. *Orthodoxy and Heterodoxy: Exploring Belief Systems Through the Lens of the Ancient Christian Faith.* Conciliar Press/Ancient Faith Publishing, 2011.

I wrote this work to compare Orthodox Christianity with other religions, mostly other forms of Christianity, though there is also a chapter on non-Christian religions. It is ostensibly addressed to Orthodox people (it was originally written as a parish educational series), but it doesn't presume knowledge of Orthodoxy in order to be read, and many non-Orthodox readers have found it a good introduction to Orthodoxy. It is arranged roughly historically, showing where various groups split off from the Orthodox faith or from each other and why.

Gallatin, Matthew. *Thirsting for God in a Land of Shallow Wells.* Conciliar Press, 2002.

Philosophy professor Matthew Gallatin was on a search to experience God, having served in the evangelical Protestant world as a musician and pastor but finding that context lacking. Only occasionally narrative in focus, this book is a good general work to introduce people from a similar background to the many ways in which Orthodoxy differs from the most common form of American Christianity. Even if the reader is a non-Christian, it will help him to see how Orthodoxy truly is different from what he might have experienced before that also wears the Christian label.

Hart, David Bentley. *Atheist Delusions: The Christian Revolution and its Fashionable Enemies.* Yale University Press, 2010.

Hart's delightfully written book is not so much a frontal attack on atheism but mainly a debunking of numerous myths that surround the history of Christianity, especially those passed around in "New Atheist" circles. Hart is himself an Orthodox Christian, but this book is not particularly an endorsement of Orthodoxy.

Hart, David Bentley. *The Experience of God: Being, Consciousness, Bliss.* Yale University Press, 2013.

This work by Hart is more of a direct address to atheism than the one above, but its purpose is, as he puts it, mainly to put forth a definition of the word *God* as used in most major religious traditions, mainly so that atheists can get some idea of what it is they're really rejecting as opposed to myths that have been constructed by unbelievers. Like *Atheist Delusions,* this book is not an apology for Orthodoxy nor really even for Christianity in general.

Louth, Andrew. *Discerning the Mystery: An Essay on the Nature of Theology.* Eighth Day Press, 2007 (reprint).

Originally published in 1983, Fr. Andrew Louth's little volume is slightly academic in its tone and makes reference to many major thinkers, but is still accessible even for those who are not as well-read as Louth is. The book is mainly a meditation on the kind of knowledge theology seeks after and why the modern faith in scientific empirical knowledge should not be exclusively placed there.

Schmemann, Alexander. *For the Life of the World: Sacraments and Orthodoxy.* St. Vladimir's Seminary Press, 1973.

This meditation on the sacramental way of life in Orthodoxy has been revolutionary for many in terms of helping them to see how God could be present in the physical world, contrary to the sensibility of secularism. I read it in the process of discovering Orthodoxy myself, and it opened my eyes to a much broader way of understanding and sensing God's grace on Earth. Schmemann was a major figure in Orthodox revitalization in the West from the 1950s until his death in 1983.

Sparks, Jack, ed. *The Apostolic Fathers.* Thomas Nelson Publishers, 1978.

There are many editions of this work, usually going by this name (the Penguin edition is called *Early Christian Writings*), but I prefer this one for its scriptural cross-references and easy readability. Contained in this volume are several works by writers who lived either during or immediately after the history recounted in the New Testament. If you want to know what Christianity looked like immediately after the Bible, this is the place to go. Most of these works are letters, but there are stories here, too. My most favorite are the letters of St. Ignatius of Antioch, who was a disciple of the Apostle John.

Webber, Meletios. *Bread & Water, Wine & Oil.* Conciliar Press/Ancient Faith Publishing, 2007.

Like Schmemann's *For the Life of the World,* Fr. Meletios's book guides the reader through a sense of the physicality of connecting with God. It is less a direct response to secularism than Schmemann's book, however, and written in a more introductory style.

Yannaras, Christos. *The Freedom of Morality*. St. Vladimir's
Seminary Press, 1996.

For those without a background in philosophy, this can
be a tough book to read, especially its first chapter, but
it's worth the work. It explains how Orthodox Christian
ethics are not really about following rules or becoming
pious Christians, but rather how morality is the free
action of a fully healed human person, energized by the
grace of God to become fully and authentically human.

Endnotes

1   Anthony Bloom, *Beginning to Pray.* Paulist Press, 1970, pp. 25–26, emphasis in original.

2   http://en.wikipedia.org/wiki/God, accessed June 13, 2014.

3   Quoted in Rivka Horwitz. *Buber's Way to "I and Thou."* Jewish Publication Society, February 1989, p. 105.

4   Cynewulf. *Christ.* Trans. Charles W. Kennedy. Cambridge, Ontario: In Parentheses Publications Old English Series, 2000, p. 4.

5   Cyprian of Carthage, *The Lord's Prayer,* 24.

6   Irenaeus, *Adversus Haereses* 4.26.2.

7   Justin Martyr, *First Apology,* 67.

8   Ignatius, *To the Philadelphians* 4.

9   *Adv. Haer.* 4.18.5.

10 Ignatius, *Smyrnaeans* 7.

11 *First Apology* 66.

12 *Adv. Haer.* 4.26.2.

13 *Adv. Haer.* 4.18.5.

14 Athanasius the Great, Letter XXXIX, 5.

15 *Adv. Haer.* 3.3.1.

16 *Adv. Haer.* 3.3.3.

17 Basil the Great, *On the Holy Spirit,* 66.

18 *The Sayings of the Desert Fathers: The Alphabetical Collection.* Trans. Benedicta Ward. Cistercian Studies Series, number 59, p. 103.

19 *Beginning to Pray,* p. 26.

20 Quoted in Rabbi Michael Leo Samuel, "Further Reflections on Buber: Where can we find the Eternal Thou?" June 2008. http://rabbimichaelsamuel. com/2008/06/further-reflections-on-buber-where-can-we-find-the-eternal-thou/

21 *Beginning to Pray,* p. 29, emphasis in original.

22 Hymn 16, George A. Maloney. *St. Symeon the New Theologian: Hymns of Divine Love.* Denville Books, NJ, 1975, p. 58.

About the Author

The Rev. Fr. Andrew Stephen Damick is pastor of St. Paul Orthodox Church in Emmaus, Pennsylvania. He also lectures widely on Orthodox evangelism, history, ecology, comparative theology, and localism. He is a founding member of the Society for Orthodox Christian History in the Americas. Fr. Andrew hosts the *Orthodoxy and Heterodoxy* and *Roads from Emmaus* podcasts, as well as writing the *Roads from Emmaus* blog and serving as editor-in-chief for the multi-author *Orthodoxy and Heterodoxy* blog. He lives in Emmaus with his wife Kh. Nicole and their children. His book *Orthodoxy and Heterodoxy* was published by Conciliar Press/Ancient Faith Publishing in 2011.

Ancient Faith Publishing hopes you have enjoyed and benefited from this book. The proceeds from the sales of our books only partially cover the costs of operating our non-profit ministry—which includes both the work of **Ancient Faith Publishing** (formerly known as Conciliar Press) and the work of **Ancient Faith Radio.** Your financial support makes it possible to continue this ministry both in print and online. Donations are tax-deductible and can be made at www.ancientfaith.com.

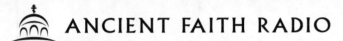

ANCIENT FAITH RADIO

Bringing you Orthodox Christian music, readings, prayers, teaching, and podcasts 24 hours a day since 2004 at
www.ancientfaith.com

The Mystery of Art

BECOMING AN ARTIST IN THE IMAGE OF GOD

by Jonathan Jackson

I

Art as Beauty

Beauty is mysterious as well as terrible. God and devil are fighting there, and the battlefield is the heart of man.

—Fyodor Dostoyevsky

God is the ultimate Artist and Poet. Being fashioned in His image means that we are also artists and poets—each one of us, regardless of our vocation in life. We are artists in the way we love each other. We are poets in the way we pray for one another—in the way we smile and weep together. Everyone is an artist. We are cosmically bound to one another through a divine tapestry that stretches across the ages. Each one of us has a unique part to play in the symphony of God's creation.

The most important work of an artist is not what he or she creates. It is in the work of being created by the grace of God. The primary focus of the artist is the working out of his salvation. What the artist creates or produces in terms of works of art is always secondary to becoming a work of art in reality. The spiritual artist continually repents his ambition and becomes the poem. This happens by sitting at the feet of the Master and beholding His glory, as the woman Mary did. The artist does not merely write or sing songs—he becomes the song. He does not simply paint on a canvas; he himself becomes a painting for the glory of God. This is a very different vision of an artist from what our culture celebrates.

Our culture says the goal of the artist is fame, recognition, and worldly glory—to receive the applause of men. Jesus Christ, who is the Image of God and of true humanity, gives an entirely different vision. He says, "Do not let your right hand know what your left hand is doing" (Matt. 6:3). In essence, He says to the artist, "Let your light shine so the world may see your good works and praise your Father who is in heaven. But as far as you are concerned, do not receive glory from people. Do these things in secret. Retreat into the closet of your heart, where ceaseless prayer resides. Remain hidden and innocent of all conceit. Your Father who sees in secret will reward you in the open."

The fallen artist pines for human applause. The spiritual artist groans for secret communion with the Creator. He knows that this only happens through *kenosis,* or self-emptying. Our society says the ultimate virtues of the artist are entertainment and monetary success. In this scheme, the artist is a means to a base materialistic end: profit and power. In contrast to this, the ultimate virtues of the spiritual artist are sanctification and transformation. In this grace-infused worldview, the artist is not only a means to these more heavenly ends, but he is also a participant in the redemption of the world itself.

BEAUTY WILL SAVE THE WORLD

The poetry of the Akathist Hymn, "Glory to God for All Things," found in the effects of Protopresbyter Gregory Petrov after his death in a Soviet prison camp in 1940, expresses the mystery of the artist:

> *In the wondrous blending of sounds it is Your call we hear; in the harmony of many voices, in the sublime beauty of music, in the glory of the works of great composers: You lead us to the threshold of paradise to come and to the choirs of angels. All true beauty has the power to draw the soul toward You and to make it sing in ecstasy: Alleluia!*

> *Ikos 7*
> *The breath of Your Holy Spirit inspires artists, poets, and scientists. The power of Your supreme knowledge makes them prophets and*

interpreters of Your laws, who reveal the depths of Your creative
wisdom. Their works speak unwittingly of You. How great are You
in Your creation! How great are You in man!

"All true beauty has the power to draw the soul toward You
and to make it sing in ecstasy: Alleluia!" Dostoyevsky would
agree with his whole heart. In his brilliant novel *The Idiot,*
the protagonist, Prince Myshkin, says, "I believe the world
will be saved by beauty. I am a believer because Christianity
is that beauty." This is the vision of the spiritual artist.

CARETAKERS OF THE CULTURE

Plato famously said, "Give me the songs of a nation, and it
matters not who writes its laws." In many ways, artists are
the caretakers of our culture. Politicians can write as many
laws as they wish, but they will never change the heart of the
culture. This belongs to the artists.

For instance, our society has become more and more violent over the past fifty years. Numerous school massacres and
random killings have left an indelible mark on our collective
psyche. Politicians continue to debate our gun-control laws.
These debates are necessary. But if our culture continues to
produce dehumanizing art that promotes the desensitiza-
tion of our youth, then it doesn't matter if our laws become
more severe. If we as a society continue to applaud artists
who produce music that is unreasonably violent, gory, or

pornographic, then we should not be surprised when we see the degradation of our culture.

It is not a matter of free speech. It is a matter of conscience. The fact that the artist is free to produce such content does not mean it is praiseworthy. The artist has an incredible influence on the zeitgeist of our culture. An artist is one of the caretakers of the spiritual health of humanity. Producing films in which pornography is depicted in a comedic manner or in which the systematic slaughter of innocent people is glorified will have an impact on the culture.

The artist is placed within this cultural dynamic to bring about the return of the prodigal world to the beauty of life. The artist is not a prude or a fundamentalist—he is not afraid to show the depths of darkness or the honesty of life. But when he is called to portray the ugliness of humanity, he will not glorify it. He will not call it beautiful or praiseworthy. He will weep as he paints and tremble as he sings. The spiritual artist will pray for the life of the world as he portrays its desperate need for healing.

THE REORIENTATION OF THE ARTIST

Beyond the art itself, I am speaking of who we are as human beings. This book is a humble exploration of human nature, as it corresponds to the image of the Eternal Artist. It is chiefly about the mystical nature of the arts and not about the practical details or methodologies of craft per se; some of these things will be touched upon, but the overarching vision of this book is the reorientation of the artist toward his eternal hearth: the Kingdom of heaven. What is art? What is man? Who is God? How do these things coincide? These are some of the questions that provide a framework for this book.

My life in the arts began at the age of eleven. I have maintained this vocation in Hollywood ever since: working in film, television, the stage, music, writing, and directing. However, I do not consider myself to be any of these things. I am not an actor. Sometimes I am called to act. I am not a musician. Sometimes I am called to play music. I am not a writer. Sometimes I am called to write. My identity is not what I do, but who I am. And who I am is a sinner embraced by the merciful Christ.

My love for each one of these artistic expressions is immense. I also love the people in these fields. My life has been deeply enriched and transformed by the grace of the artists I have been privileged to work with. My heart has been moved in countless ways through the creative and spiritual interaction with my mad coworkers. It is important to stress that there are many artists who do not consciously share these religious convictions and yet possess a radiant grace and participation in the truths of traditional Christianity. Christ is "all and in all" (Col. 3:11), and I do not wish to project any triumphalism in this book. Christlike humility is the way of the artist.

THE BEAUTY OF SYNERGY

The first time I succeeded in persuading my brother Richard to play the drums while I jammed on the guitar was an unforgettable moment. I was eleven years old and he was fourteen. I had been playing guitar for three years, and he had been playing drums off and on since he was seven. Strangely, we had never played together. I had tried many times to coerce him to play with me, but he wouldn't budge. He just wasn't interested. Why would anyone want to play with his little brother, anyway? I get it. But, somehow, I finally persuaded him. We had a basement with a drum set, and I brought my guitar down there and plugged it into a cheap amplifier.

What occurred over the next half-hour was astonishing, for us at least. It was as if the ceiling of our basement opened up and the sky itself radiated upon us. The noise! The adrenaline! The energy! The music! It was actual music! We both looked at each other, utterly amazed—did that just happen? Is that even possible?

Now, I'm fully aware that the objective quality of what we were playing was probably not very impressive, but to us, it was magnificent. Something shifted within us that day. The proof is that twenty years later we're still playing music together and dreaming of how to create powerful and moving songs to share with people. What happened in that basement was a creative encounter. My instrument encountered his instrument, and something profound took place. It was the power of synergy. I loved playing the guitar, but it was nothing compared to playing the guitar while Richard hammered away on those drums. That was tremendous. That was the beginning of something: a flame that would not be easy to douse.

Why are moments like this so powerful? I believe it is because humanity is stumbling upon something beautiful: a mystery of our true nature. Creating is the art of encountering the beauty of life. Humanity was created in the Image of God.